SHENANIGAMES

Grammar-Focused Interactive ESL/EFL Activities and Games

James Kealey
Donna Inness

PRO LINGUA ⬤ **ASSOCIATES**

Pro Lingua Associates, Publishers
P.O. Box 1348
Brattleboro, Vermont 05302 USA
Office: 802 257 7779
Orders: 800 366 4775
Webstore: www.ProLinguaAssociates.com
E-mail: info@ProLinguaAssociates.com
        orders@ProLinguaAssociates.com
SAN 216-0579

At Pro Lingua,
our objective is to foster an approach
to learning and teaching that we call
interplay, the interaction of language
learners and teachers with their materials,
with the language and culture,
and with each other in active, creative,
and productive play.

This book was designed and set in Times text, Akzidenz Grotesk display, and a variety of other types by Judy Ashkenaz of Total Concept Associates and Arthur A. Burrows in Brattleboro, Vermont. The book was printed and bound by Sheridan Books of Fredericksburg, Virginia.

Most of the illustrations are by the authors. Other graphic elements are from *Art Explosion 125,000 Images*, © 1996 by Nova Development Corporation. The maps in The Great Modal Race are from MapArt © 1994 by Cartesia. Cartoons used in Canned Bingo, Sharing Should, and The Great Modal Chase are from *Task Force Clip Art for Macintosh*, © 1994 by New Vision Technologies, Inc.

Printed in the United States of America.
Fourth printing 2006   7000 in print

Contents

Contents, continued

Preface

The purpose of this book is to provide a collection of communicative activities that encourage students to interact with one another while practicing key grammar points in English. Recognizing the roles that challenge and confidence-building play in successful language learning, we have designed two types of activities. The first provides students with the grammatical forms, while the second requires students to produce them. Both types include cooperative task-solving and opinion-sharing activities. All are student-driven and require minimal teacher input, permitting the instructor to assume the role of observer and facilitator after introducing the activity.

Although this is not a grammar textbook, the activities are grouped according to grammar focus for ease of reference. They are appropriate as supplementary exercises in an ESL grammar or listening/speaking class at the high school, college, or adult level.

Because this is a supplementary text, we encourage teachers to choose and adapt the material to fit individual course needs. We offer the following suggestions:

1. Choose activities based on factors such as grammar currently being taught, time constraints, and students' language level and interests. Many of the exercises in this book are in game format. Although experience has proved these games to be successful and motivating for many students, we realize that classes have their own "group personality," and what will work well in one class may be less successful in another.

2. Identify unfamiliar vocabulary and preteach it.

3. Modify instructions as necessary. For example, we have used grammatical labels such as "participles." Change them if your students don't know these terms.

4. Adjust activities to suit class size. For example, if your class is larger than the suggested size for a particular activity, divide the students into two groups and run simultaneous games.

5. Decide when a game is completed—for example, when a certain number of points is obtained, when a predetermined time period has elapsed, or when a given number of rounds has been played.

We hope these activities will add to the ESL teacher's repertoire and contribute to the students' enjoyment and success in learning English.

James Kealey
Donna Inness

A Note on Appropriate Age Ranges and Proficiency Levels

If your students enjoy learning by playing games, most of the game techniques in this book can be adapted for use with students of almost any age and a proficiency range from advanced elementary to advanced intermediate. Most students do eventually enjoy classroom games, but it is important not to make older students feel that you are talking down to them or treating them like children. If some of your students seem to be put off when you first introduce these games, take some time to let them relax and become more comfortable with you and their fellow students. Then, when you reintroduce games, be sure to start with one that practices skills and vocabulary that are immediately relevant and that does not require childish behavior.

The grammar-focused games in this book have been written for use with adults. They can be useful in all kinds of high school, adult education, and university preparation English language programs, both in the U.S. and overseas. Many of the games could even be used as is with middle school students, depending on the maturity of the class. However, if the game as it is presented here seems inappropriate, **we encourage you to adapt it**. Any of the techniques may work well with different vocabulary and graphics more appropriate to your class. Although we have developed photocopyable materials for the games, at heart "the technique's the thing," and we hope it will provide your classes with some entertainment as well as valuable practice with the grammar in question.

The proficiency level appropriate for any of these games varies. If your students' conversational English is strong enough to be able to enjoy the game, it is appropriate to use it as long as they need to practice the grammar. Some elementary students (not absolute beginners) will find these games very helpful; others would be overwhelmed. At the other extreme, some advanced intermediate students need to focus on grammar, and these games provide a relatively painless way to practice; for other students with strong grammar backgrounds, these games would be inappropriate. You, the teacher, are the best judge.

Editor's Pronouncement on Pronouns

In this book, we at Pro Lingua Associates offer a solution to the vexing *he/she* pronoun problem. We have decided that when a reference is made to a third-person singular person, and that person is indefinite (and hence gender is unknown or unimportant), we will use the third-person plural forms *they, them, their(s)*.

We are fully aware that historically these forms represent grammatical plurality. However, there are clear instances in the English language where the third-person plural form is used to refer to a preceding indefinite, grammatically singular pronoun. Here are some examples:

> **Everyone says this, don't** *they?*
> **Nobody agrees with us, but we will ignore** *them.*

If you will accept the examples above, it is not a major step to find the following acceptable:

> **The learner of English should find this easier because** *they* **can avoid the confusion of** *he* **or** *she,* **the awkwardness of** *he or she,* **and the implicit sexism of using** *he* **for everybody.**

So in this book you will find instructions such as:

> **If a student touches the wrong color,** *they* **have to sit down.**

The reader may disagree with our solution, but we ask them to blame us, the publishers, not the author.

Languages do change, and the English language needs to change its usage of gender-marked pronouns when they are clearly inappropriate. This is our solution. We encourage you to try it out, and we invite your comments.

—RCC for PLA

Grammar-Focused SHENANIGAMES

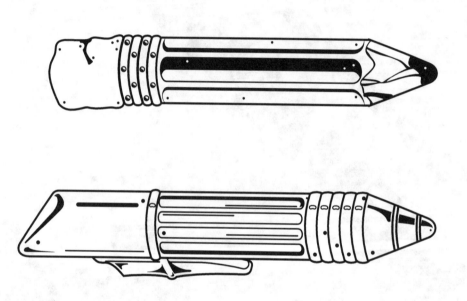

Matched Adjectives

Language Focus

Adjectives.

Summary of Game

Each team is given a noun, and each student gets 5 minutes to write a list of adjectives describing that noun. After 5 minutes, the members compare their lists, and the team with the greatest number of duplicate adjectives wins.

Number of Players

Ideally, two or more teams of 4 or 5 students each.

Preparation by Teacher

Before Class
Gather a supply of large index cards or similar sheets of paper. If one of the students will be choosing the nouns the teams will use, make a copy of the **Nouns** list.

In Class
1. Divide the class into teams.
2. Give each student a sheet or paper or a large index card.
3. Announce or write on the board a noun from the list below.

Directions to Students

1. You will be given a noun and a piece of paper.
2. Write as many adjectives that describe the noun as you can think of in five minutes.
3. Compare your lists. Your team will get one point for each adjective that matches a classmate's.
4. For example, if your noun is *tree* and two students on your team write *green,* your team gets two points.
5. The team with the most points after five minutes wins.

Matched Adjectives
Nouns

elephant	shoe	beer
student	beach	friend
teacher	wall	ocean
rose	English	mother
cat	telephone	peanut butter
sports car	monkey	Hawaii
hamburger	politician	clock
children	blanket	morning
snake	ice cream	computer
golf	milk	neckties
city	Michael Jackson	airplanes
autumn	Beethoven	kitchen
dictionary	moon	doctor
exam	hair	gun
cloud	tree	brother

Tiger Hunt

Language Focus

Adjectives, practice with yes/no questions.

Summary of Game

The class is divided into three teams, A, B, and C. Each team chooses a noun and adjectives from lists supplied by the teacher. The other teams try to guess, to "hunt down" those nouns and adjectives by asking yes/no questions.

Number of Players

Any number divided into three teams of hunters.

Preparation by Teacher

1. You need lists of nouns and adjectives, a timer, and several pieces of paper.
2. Divide the class into three teams.
3. Give each student on each team a list of nouns and a list of "matching" adjectives. You can use the lists on the following pages. Choose a list that seems appropriate to the level of the students. Give the students the following directions. Stress the importance of keeping their group decisions secret and of limiting questions to the yes/no variety that do not use the adjectives directly.

Directions to Students

1. Team A is given a list of nouns and a list of adjectives.
2. Being very careful not to be overheard, Team A chooses an interesting noun, like *tiger*. Then they choose two or more adjectives that exemplify that noun, like *striped* and *yellow*.
3. Next they write their noun on a piece of paper and give it and the complete list of adjectives to the hunters on Team B.
4. Team B then has 3 minutes to guess the two or more adjectives by asking the members of Team A as many yes/no questions as they can. They are not allowed to use the adjectives directly. For example, they might ask, "Does this thing have a color? Is that color dark red?" Team C stays out of the room.
5. If they succeed in guessing the adjectives, Team B then writes them on a piece of paper and gives them to Team C.
6. The teacher or someone on Team A then times Team C as the members try to guess the original noun within 5 minutes.
7. When this round of questions is over, the teacher gives the lists of nouns and adjectives to Team B and then to Team C. Again, only yes/no questions that do not use the adjectives directly are allowed.
8. The winning team is the one that either hunts down the original noun in the least amount of time or scares up the most adjectives in the 3 minutes allowed.

Tiger Hunt

Nouns

dog	volcano	fox
cow	microwave	box
crow	CD	politician
bus	tiger	cookbook
tub	circus	bathing beauty
tank	clown	life guard
clock	cannon	college student
restaurant	cat	businesswoman
cab	high school	mail carrier
elevator	soccer team	druggist
subway	box of Wheaties	calendar
notebook	opera	time machine
station wagon	ballerina	Martian
play	living room	greenhouse
movie	kitchenette	dessert
novel	castle	arm chair
wolf	army	suitcase
time machine	hero	music box
sweater	piano	board of education

Tiger Hunt

Common Adjectives

active	delicious	sharp
black	fierce	slippery
blond	fragrant	slow
bright	green	small
bubbly	hard	soft
careless	high	sour
cheerful	hot	spotted
comfortable	juicy	sweet
curly	long	tall
curved	loud	weak
dangerous	mushy	wet
dark	red	white

Section: Adjectives

Tiger Hunt

Less Common Adjectives

absorbent	edible	luminous
acrobatic	entertaining	metallic
adorable	ferocious	moist
angry	funny	monotonous
animated	furry	oval
aromatic	gloomy	plump
black	glossy	poisonous
bouncing	greasy	reliable
brand-new	green	striped
bulky	hideous	thick
cold	idle	ugly
colorful	inedible	valuable
cozy	informative	wrinkled
creamy	large	yellow
docile	low	young

Face It!

Language Focus

Adjectives describing facial expressions and emotions.

Summary of Game

Students think of possible reasons for pictured emotions, then try to figure out whose emotions their classmates describe to them.

Number of Players

1-20.

Preparation by Teacher

Before Class
1. Copy **Numbers and Names.**
2. Cut out and use as many of the 20 slips as you have students. Shuffle those slips.
3. Make one copy of **Faces** for each student.

In Class
1. Give each student a **Numbers and Names** slip. Remind them not to let anyone else see it.
2. Give each student a copy of **Faces.**

Directions to Students

Phase One
1. Each of you has a slip with a **Number and Name**, and a page of **Faces**. The numbers next to the **Faces** correspond to those on the **Number and Name** slips.
2. The **Faces** show various expressions. Look at the **Face** of your person. Think about the emotion that person is showing.
3. Imagine what event caused or is causing that emotion or expression.
4. Put your idea in a sentence. (You may memorize it or write it on your slip of paper.) Don't describe the look, just the event. For example, *don't* say, "Bobby's *sad* because his cat just died." Say, "Bobby's cat just died."

Phase Two (after students have had time to prepare their sentences)
1. Circulate, telling classmates your sentence.
2. Listen to their sentences. Try to figure out whose **Faces** they describe.
3. The first person to identify all the **Faces** correctly wins.

1. Ricky	2. Caroline
3. Sam	4. Mickey
5. Becky	6. Carlos
7. Jill	8. Lionel
9. Billy	10. Trina
11. Lois	12. Mark
13. Jerry	14. Julie
15. Betsy	16. Kyle
17. Shauna	18. Travis
19. Nick	20. Michelle

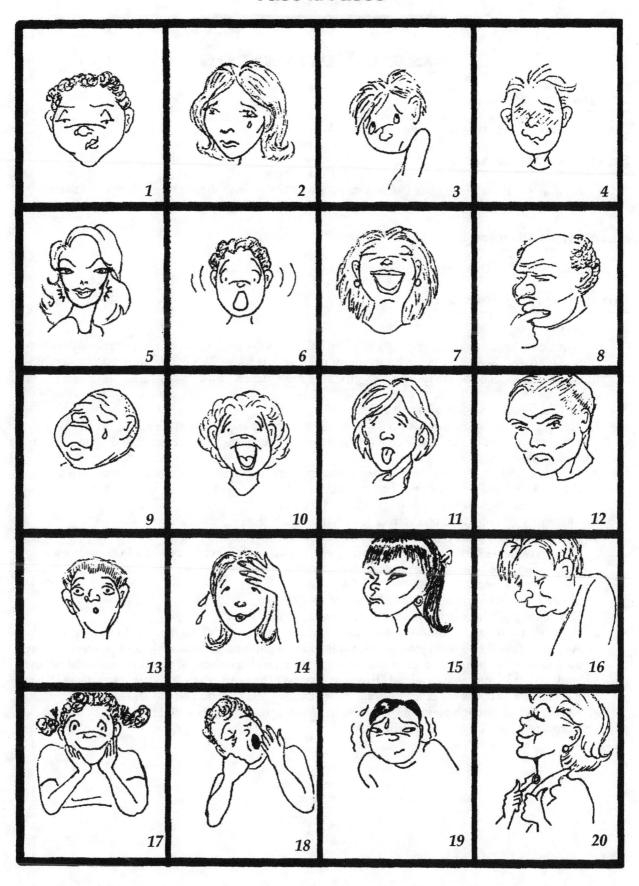

 Section: Adjectives

Jigsaw Sentences

Language Focus

Word order, relative clauses, punctuation.

Summary of Game

Holding cards containing parts of a sentence, students arrange themselves in a row so that their cards form a logical sentence.

Number of Players

Minimum of 8. There are a possible 15 parts given for each sentence.

Preparation by Teacher

Before Class
Using only large capital letters, copy onto separate cards or pieces of paper each word and punctuation mark of a sentences given on the **Sentence Fragments** sheet. (Words with asterisks are optional. They can be added for use with groups of more than 8.) Shuffle the cards.

In Class (with classes of up to 15)
1. This game is played by the class as a whole unless there are 16 or more students, in which case they can play with two teams of at least 8 each. Give each student a card, face down, telling them not to look at their cards.
2. At your signal, the students look at their cards and move around discussing their cards until they're able to stand in a row with their cards forming a logical sentence. When they are finished, the students read their sentence aloud. Time this process.
3. There may be more than one correct sentence for each group of words below.
4. The class can try to beat their own time with new sentences.
5. If you have more cards than students, you can give two cards to some students. In order to stand in line forming the sentence, they will probably have to give *one* card away to someone else.

Team Play (recommended for classes of 16 or more)
1. Divide the class into teams of at least 8 students each.
2. Have one team stand. Hand one card to each student, face down. Tell them not to look at their cards.
3. At your signal, the students look at their cards and move around discussing their cards until they are able to stand in a row with their cards forming a logical sentence. When they are finished, the students read their sentence aloud. Time this process. The other team(s) watch. After the sentence has been formed, ask the other students if they can suggest variation on the sentence.
4. Repeat steps 1 through 3 with the other team(s) forming new sentences while the first team watches. Compare times. The fastest team wins.

Directions to Students

1. Each of you has a card with a word or a punctuation mark. Don't look at the card or show it to anyone else until I give you the signal to begin.

2. When I say, "Begin," look at your card, and then, working together, arrange yourselves so that you use all the cards to form a correct sentence. Don't hand your cards to anyone else. (If you have two cards, you may give *one* of them to another student.) I will time you. When you think your sentence is correct, read it aloud.

3a. *(for one team)* When you're finished, I will give you a chance to beat your own time with a new sentence.

3b. *(for two teams)* When you're finished, I will give the other team(s) a chance to beat your time with a new sentence.

Jigsaw Sentences
Sentence Fragments

THE   TWO-STORY*   HOUSE   WHERE   CHRIS   AND*   TERRY*   BROWN*   GREW   UP   WAS   TORN   DOWN   LAST*   WEEK* .

THE   TALL*   ,*   RED-HAIRED*   MAN   WITH   WHOM   SHE   ATE   DINNER   IS   MY*   BROTHER*   ,*   PAUL .

HOW   DO   YOU   ARGUE   EFFECTIVELY*   WITH   SOMEONE   WHO   DOESN'T   LISTEN   TO*   ANYTHING*   YOU*   SAY*   ?

JENNIFER   ,*   MY*   FRIEND*   ,*   HAS*   TOLD   ME   SOME-THING   INTERESTING*   THAT   I   SHOULD   KEEP   SECRET .

WE   THANKED   THE   GRACIOUS*   ,*   ELDERLY*   COUPLE   IN   WHOSE   SUMMER*   COTTAGE   WE   STAYED   LAST*   JUNE* .

IT   WAS   NOT*   RAINING   HEAVILY*   ON   THE   APRIL*   DAY   I   MET   YOU   AND*   YOUR*   SON* .

IT*   IS*   A*   WISE*   OLD*   SAYING*   THAT*   HE   WHO   HAS   NOTHING   HAS   NOTHING   TO   LOSE .

Eric's Schedule

Language Focus

Adverb phrases and clauses of time.

Summary of Game

Each student is given a slip of paper on which is a statement describing one of Eric's activities in relation to the time at which he did something else. The students are also given a blank schedule for Eric's afternoon between 4:00 and 8:00 P.M. Their object is to fill in Eric's schedule by putting his activities in the correct order.

Number of Players

There are 11 activities described, so the game can be played with up to 11 students. If fewer students play, each will have more than one statement to work with. The game can also be played with two or more teams of at least 4 students each.

Preparation by Teacher

Before Class
1. Make one copy of the blank schedule for each team, or draw one on the board.
2. Make a copy of the statements for each team and cut it into strips, each describing one activity.

In Class
1. Divide the class into teams of at least 4 students each.
2. Give each team a schedule and a complete set of 11 statements.

Directions to Students

1. Each of you has one or more statements telling something that Eric did between 4:00 and 8:00 P.M. yesterday.
2. Read your statement out loud to your teammates.
3. Working together, find the logical order of the statements and fill in Eric's schedule using all of his activities.
4. If you have more than one team, the first team to complete Eric's schedule correctly wins the game.

Solution

4:00	groomed pet pig	memorized French vocabulary list
5:00	practiced karate kicks	
6:00	trimmed the hedge	
7:00	shaved head	listened to radio
8:00	worked on his shoelace collection	talked on phone

As soon as he finished trimming the hedge, he shaved his head.

After grooming his pet pig, he practiced his karate kicks.

He didn't listen to the radio while he was practicing his karate kicks.

He didn't memorize his French vocabulary list during his work on his shoelace collection.

He listened to the radio before he talked on the phone.

He didn't work on his shoelace collection before talking on the phone.

He shaved his head sometime after he practiced his karate kicks.

He listened to the radio after he memorized his French vocabulary list.

He didn't talk on the phone before working on his shoelace collection.

He listened to the radio right after he had trimmed the hedge.

Just before practicing his karate kicks, he memorized his French vocabulary list.

ERIC'S SCHEDULE

TIME	ACTIVITIES	ACTIVITIES
4:00		
5:00		
6:00		
7:00		
8:00		

"Where Were You When ...?"

Language Focus

Adverb phrases and clauses of time.

Summary of Game

Students solve a murder mystery based on clues taken from players' alibis.

Number of Players

9–13. There are 9 essential characters and 4 optional characters to be used with a larger class.

Preparation by Teacher

Before Class

1. Make a copy of the **Investigator's Report** (page 18) sheet for each student.
2. Make a copy of the sheet of **Alibi Statements**.
3. Each student will play the role of a murder suspect. Assign a student's name to each character, replacing the lettered blanks in the **Alibi Statements** with the name. Cut the sheet of statements into strips along the dotted lines and give the statements to the students to whom they have been assigned.

In Class

1. Give each student a copy of the **Investigator's Report** sheet and one **Alibi Statement**, with the student's name. If you choose to use the group format described below, have the students sit in a circle.
2. Read the **Scene**, below, to the class.

Directions to Students

Group Format

Each of you is a murder suspect who has an alibi to account for your activities at the time of the murder. Memorize your alibi. As we go around the circle, you will state your alibis. The group will listen to each statement and try to identify the murderer by detecting the inconsistent alibi.

Competitive Format

Each of you is a murder suspect who has an alibi to account for your activities at the time of the murder. Memorize your alibi. Circulate around the room asking other suspects for their alibis. The first student to identify the murderer by detecting the inconsistent alibi wins the game. Use the **Investigator's Report** sheet you have been given to help keep track of the alibis.

Scene

Between 4:00 and 4:30 on Saturday afternoon, Mr. Smith was murdered. All the boarders in Mr. Smith's boarding house are suspects.

Solution

D is the murderer. D's alibi is inconsistent with G's and J's statements about the paper delivery.

(A)_____: After watching baseball on TV for a couple of hours, I went to the basement to play Ping-Pong with (B)_____ shortly after 4:30.

(B)_____: Before playing Ping-Pong, I took a nap from 4:00 to 4:30.

(C)_____: I took a shower at 4 o'clock. As soon as I finished, I got a phone call from my friend, and we talked for about an hour.

(D)_____: At about 4 o'clock, I noticed the newspaper on the coffee table in the den. I read it until 5:00, when I went to Burger Palace.

(E)_____: I went out to mow the lawn at 4:00. While mowing the front lawn, I noticed (G)_____ and (J) _____ sitting on the porch of the boarding house.

(F)_____: At 4 o'clock I was playing chess with (H)_____. Sometime during the game—I think it was about 4:45—I answered the phone. It was a call for (C)_____.

(G)_____: (J)_____ and I fixed ourselves a quick supper and took it out to the front porch. While we were eating dessert, I noticed that the paper hadn't been delivered yet. Surprised, I looked at my watch; it was 4:50.

(H)_____: (F)_____ and I played chess in my room all afternoon until about 6:00, when we went downstairs for supper. During the game we heard loud voices coming from Smith's bedroom.

(J) _____: (G)_____ and I had dinner on the front porch. I had just finished eating when the paper was delivered. I took it into the house and left it on the coffee table on my way to the kitchen with the dirty dishes.

OPTIONAL CHARACTERS (FOR LARGER CLASSES):

(K) _____: I was weeding the garden while (F) was cutting the grass.

(L) _____: After lunch I went down to the tennis courts to play a few sets with (M) _____. After the match we stopped at Burger Palace for a quick supper.

(M)_____: I beat (L)_____ at four sets of tennis. Afterwards, we grabbed a bite at Burger Palace, where we ran into (D) _____.

(N)_____: I spent the day in _____ at my sister's wedding. I
                                                    (nearby city)
didn't get back to the house until 8:00.

Official
Investigator's Report Sheet

Investigator's name:

Date of investigation:

Below, take notes on the alibi of each of the suspects.

Suspect 1. Name:
Alibi:

Suspect 8. Name:
Alibi:

Suspect 2. Name:
Alibi:

Suspect 9. Name:
Alibi:

Suspect 3. Name:
Alibi:

Suspect 10. Name:
Alibi:

Suspect 4. Name:
Alibi:

Suspect 11. Name:
Alibi:

Suspect 5. Name:
Alibi:

Suspect 12. Name:
Alibi:

Suspect 6. Name:
Alibi:

Suspect 13. Name:
Alibi:

Suspect 7. Name:
Alibi:

Other observations:

Signature of the investigator:

An Article's Article

Language Focus

Articles *a, an, the,* and #. Focused listening skills and reading aloud.

Summary of Game

Students listen to a story read by another student, and they indicate the correct missing articles on a score card.

Number of Players

Any number.

Preparation by Teacher

Before Class

1. Make one copy of the **Article Score Card** for each student plus two extras for you and the **Reader** to use in recording the players' answers and deciding the winning team. Make a copy of the **Answers** for the **Reader**.
2. The **Article** can be read from this book, but it may be more convenient to use a copy.

In Class

1. Divide the class into two teams, and then give each player an **Article Score Card**.
2. Choose a student **Reader**. Give them the **Article** beforehand and explain what they are to do. Ask them to read fairly slowly and, when reading aloud, to say "bleep" fairly quietly, pausing slightly after the sound. This comes naturally if they pop (accentuate) the *p*. This adds to the humor without obscuring the story: "It was *bleeP* (pause) night before Christmas …"

   If reading aloud is too difficult for your students, consider either reading the story aloud yourself or giving it to them as a reading exercise. They read the story and mark down the answers on the score card. Then you count their answers as explained above. After adding up the results, you announce the winning team.

Directions to Students

1. This is your **Reader**. She/he will read you a story, a magazine **Article**. All the articles have been left out, and the **Reader** will substitute the sound *bleep* for the missing articles—for example, "I'd like *bleep* Coke, please." If you don't understand your **Reader**, say, "Please repeat that."
2. You each have an **Article Score Card**. When you hear a *bleep*, decide what article is needed in that place. Mark your decision on your **Score Card**—an *a*, an *an*, a *the*, or silence, indicated by the # (pound sign). In some cases, more than one answer is possible. You will know which number to mark because the **Reader** will read a number after the phrase and give you a second to mark your score card: "I'd like *bleep* Coke, please (6)."
3. After we have finished listening to the **Article** and filling out the **Score Card**, the **Reader** and we will ask you for your answers ("Everyone with *the* raise your hand"), and we'll count them. We will then add up the correct answers, tell you what is correct, and announce the winning team—the one with the most correct answers.

Articles Article Score Card

1. __ a, __an, __the, __#   14. __ a, __an, __the, __#

2. __ a, __an, __the, __#   15. __ a, __an, __the, __#

3. __ a, __an, __the, __#   16. __ a, __an, __the, __#

4. __ a, __an, __the, __#   17. __ a, __an, __the, __#

5. __ a, __an, __the, __#   18. __ a, __an, __the, __#

6. __ a, __an, __the, __#   19. __ a, __an, __the, __#

7. __ a, __an, __the, __#   20. __ a, __an, __the, __#

8. __ a, __an, __the, __#   21. __ a, __an, __the, __#

9. __ a, __an, __the, __#   22. __ a, __an, __the, __#

10. __ a, __an, __the, __#   23. __ a, __an, __the, __#

11. __ a, __an, __the, __#   24. __ a, __an, __the, __#

12. __ a, __an, __the, __#   25. __ a, __an, __the, __#

13. __ a, __an, __the, __#   26. __ a, __an, __the, __#

Irish couple win Megabucks

BOSTON, Mass. (AP) – *Bleep* Irish couple *(1)* won more than $3.5 million in *bleep* Massachusetts Megabucks lottery *(2)*, *bleep* officials said Tuesday night *(3)*.

Bleep winners *(4)* were Ralph Murphy, 36, *bleep* unemployed house painter *(5)*, and his wife Elizabeth, 34, *bleep* waitress, also unemployed *(6)*. They live in *bleep* town of Quincy *(7)*. *Bleep* couple won exactly $3,578,640 *(8)*.

"I was so broke last week," Mrs. Murphy said. "I couldn't pay *bleep* rent *(9)*. I can't get over it. I'm not used to this kind of money. It's like *bleep* friend's death *(10)*. *Bleep* reality hasn't set in yet *(11)*.

After paying *bleep* taxes *(12)*, they will receive *bleep* checks *(13)* for $134,199 each year for 20 years, according to David Ellis of *bleep* Massachusetts State Lottery Commission *(14)*.

They bought *bleep* ticket *(15)* at *bleep* liquor store in Quincy *(16)*. *Bleep* machine shown live on TV Tuesday night *(17)* picked *bleep* lucky number *(18)*.

Bleep Murphys *(19)* came to *bleep* U.S. five years ago *(20)*. They are now in *bleep* country illegally *(21)*. They have applied for *bleep* visas *(22)*, but they do not know if they will receive them.

Bleep couple have two children *(23)* and are expecting *bleep* third in March *(24)*.

According to Ellis, *bleep* family *(25)* will be able to keep *bleep* lottery money *(26)* even if they are deported.

Articles Article Answers

1. __ a, X̲ an, __ the, __ #   14. __ a, __ an, X̲ the, __ #

2. __ a, __ an, X̲ the, __ #   15. __ a, __ an, X̲ the, __ #

3. __ a, __ an, __ the, X̲ #   16. X̲ a, __ an, __ the, __ #

4. __ a, __ an, X̲ the, __ #   17. X̲ a, __ an, __ the, __ #

5. __ a, X̲ an, __ the, __ #   18. __ a, __ an, X̲ the, __ #

6. X̲ a, __ an, __ the, __ #   19. __ a, __ an, X̲ the, __ #

7. __ a, __ an, X̲ the, __ #   20. __ a, __ an, X̲ the, __ #

8. __ a, __ an, X̲ the, __ #   21. __ a, __ an, X̲ the, __ #

9. __ a, __ an, X̲ the, __ #   22. __ a, __ an, __ the, X̲ #

10. X̲ a, __ an, __ the, __ #   23. __ a, __ an, X̲ the, __ #

11. __ a, __ an, X̲ the, X̲ #   24. X̲ a, __ an, __ the, __ #

12. __ a, __ an, X̲ the, X̲ #   25. __ a, __ an, X̲ the, __ #

13. __ a, __ an, __ the, X̲ #   26. __ a, __ an, X̲ the, __ #

Speed Search

Language Focus

Comparatives, superlatives.

Summary of Game

Students circulate to see how many people they can find who fit the descriptions on slips of paper they have drawn.

Number of Players

2–26. There are 26 slips with descriptions.

Preparation by Teacher

Before Class

1. Make a copy of the **Descriptions**.
2. Cut the slips apart along the dotted lines and place them in a box.

Directions to Students

1. Each of you will draw one slip of paper from the box.
2. By questioning your classmates and teacher, find as many people as you can who fit the description on your slip of paper. You'll have 2 minutes. (Time may be shortened for smaller classes.) You'll receive 1 point for each name.
3. When the 2 minutes are up, draw another slip of paper and continue as before. After all the rounds have been played (the teacher determines the number of rounds), the student with the most points wins.

FIND PEOPLE WITH CARS OLDER THAN THREE YEARS OLD.

FIND PEOPLE WHO ARE THE OLDEST CHILDREN IN THEIR FAMILIES.

FIND PEOPLE WHO HAVE MORE THAN $2 WITH THEM.

FIND PEOPLE WHO HAVE MORE THAN TWO BROTHERS.

FIND PEOPLE WHO HAVE LESS THAN $3 ON THEM.

FIND PEOPLE WHO HAVE FEWER THAN THREE SISTERS.

FIND PEOPLE WHO ARE THE SHORTEST IN THEIR IMMEDIATE FAMILIES.

FIND PEOPLE WHOSE SHOES ARE SMALLER THAN YOURS ARE.

FIND PEOPLE WHO HAVE MORE THAN TWO PETS.

FIND PEOPLE WHO ARE FROM THE LARGEST CITIES IN THEIR COUNTRIES.

FIND PEOPLE WHO HAVE BEEN IN THIS TOWN LONGER THAN SIX MONTHS.

FIND PEOPLE WHO ARE TALLER THAN 5'6".

FIND PEOPLE WHO USE A COMPUTER MORE FREQUENTLY THAN ONCE A WEEK.

Section: Comparisons   24

FIND PEOPLE WHO THINK THAT EDDIE MURPHY IS FUNNIER THAN ROBIN WILLIAMS.

FIND PEOPLE WHO THINK WINTER IS BETTER THAN SUMMER.

FIND PEOPLE IN WHOSE COUNTRIES GAS IS MORE EXPENSIVE THAN IT IS IN THE U.S.

FIND PEOPLE WHO THINK COMEDIES ARE LESS INTERESTING THAN THRILLER MOVIES.

FIND PEOPLE WHO CONSIDER BEAUTIFUL EYES MORE ATTRACTIVE THAN BEAUTIFUL HAIR.

FIND PEOPLE WHO BELIEVE THAT DOGS ARE LESS INTELLIGENT THAN CATS.

FIND PEOPLE WHO THINK THAT THEIR LEGS ARE THE MOST MUSCULAR PARTS OF THEIR BODIES.

FIND PEOPLE WHO THINK THAT THEY ARE THE MOST SERIOUS MEMBERS OF THEIR FAMILIES.

FIND PEOPLE IN WHOSE COUNTRIES THE WEATHER IS COLDER THAN IT IS IN THE COLDEST PARTS OF THE UNITED STATES.

FIND PEOPLE WHO THINK MATH IS MORE INTERESTING THAN HISTORY.

FIND PEOPLE WHO THINK THAT GOLF IS MORE CHALLENGING THAN TENNIS.

FIND PEOPLE WHO THINK THAT PROFESSIONAL SOCCER PLAYERS SHOULD GET HIGHER SALARIES THAN NURSES.

FIND PEOPLE WHO THINK THAT CATS ARE NICER PETS THAN DOGS.

Comparative Trivia

Language Focus

Comparative forms of adjectives and adverbs.

Summary of Game

Students decide whether comparisons made by other class members are true or false.

Number of Players

Any number.

Preparation by Teacher

Before Class
Make a copy of the **Comparative Trivia Activity Sheet** and the **Comparative Trivia Score Card** for each student.

In Class
1. Seat the students in a circle. (In classes of more than 13, form two circles.)
2. Give each student a copy of the **Comparative Trivia Activity Sheet** and the **Comparative Trivia Score Card**.
3. Assign each student a number from 1 to 13.

Directions to Students

1. You have been assigned a number. Look at your number on the **Comparative Trivia Activity Sheet**. You'll find two noun phrases and an adjective or an adverb.
2. Write a sentence comparing the two noun phrases, using the correct form of the adjective or adverb. You can make your sentence positive or negative, true or false. There are four possibilities.
3. Read your sentence to your classmates. They'll listen carefully and then mark on their **Comparative Trivia Score Card** whether your sentence is TRUE or FALSE, according to their opinion.
4. After all of the statements have been made, the teacher will give the two answers that are true, each worth one point. The student with the most points for recognizing true answers wins.

Comparative Trivia
Activity Sheet

EXAMPLE:

the Amazon River   T   F
the Mississippi River
is short   —— ——

POSSIBLE ANSWERS:
The Mississippi River is shorter than the Amazon River. (T)
The Amazon River is shorter than the Mississippi River. (F)
The Mississippi is not shorter than the Amazon River. (F)
The Amazon River is not shorter than the Mississippi River. (T)

---

1. New York City
   Mexico City
   is large

2. the temperature in the middle of the earth
   the temperature on the surface of the sun
   is hot

3. boxing
   golf
   is old

4. a pig
   an elephant
   lives long

5. a Mercedes
   a Maserati
   is expensive

6. the Dead Sea in Jordan
   Death Valley in California
   is deep

7. a kangaroo
   a wolf
   runs fast

8. Japan
   Puerto Rico
   is small

9. 20 degrees C.
   50 degrees F.
   is warm

10. one mile
    two kilometers
    is long

11. television
    the telephone
    was invented recently

12. an orange
    a banana
    has few calories

13. a zebra
    an alligator
    weighs little

        Section: Comparisons

Comparative Trivia
Activity Sheet Answers

1. Mexico City is larger than New York City. (T)
New York City is larger than Mexico City. (F)
Mexico City isn't larger than New York City, (F)
New York City isn't larger than Mexico City (T)

2. The temperature in the center of the earth is hotter
than the temperature on the surface of the sun. (T)
The temperature on the surface of the sun is hotter
than the temperature in the center of the earth. (F)
The temperature in the center of the earth isn't hotter
than the temperature on the surface of the sun. (F)
The temperature on the surface of the sun isn't hotter
than the temperature in the center of the earth. (T)

3. Boxing is older than golf. (T)
Golf is older than boxing. (F)
Boxing isn't older than golf. (F)
Golf isn't older than boxing. (T)

4. An elephant lives longer than a pig. (T)
A pig lives longer than an elephant. (F)
An elephant doesn't live longer than a pig. (F)
A pig doesn't live longer than an elephant. (T)

5. A Maserati is more expensive than a Mercedes. (T)
A Mercedes is more expensive than a Maserati. (F)
A Maserati isn't more expensive than a Mercedes. (F)
A Mercedes isn't more expensive than a Maserati. (T)

6. The Dead Sea in Jordan is deeper than Death
Valley in California. (T)
Death Valley in California is deeper than the Dead
Sea in Jordan. (F)
The Dead Sea in Jordan isn't deeper than Death
Valley in California. (F)
Death Valley in California isn't deeper than the Dead
Sea in Jordan. (T)

7. A kangaroo runs faster than a wolf. (T)
A wolf runs faster than a kangaroo. (F)
A kangaroo doesn't run faster than a wolf. (F)
A wolf doesn't run faster than a kangaroo. (T)

8. Puerto Rico is smaller than Japan. (T)
Japan is smaller than Puerto Rico. (F)
Puerto Rico isn't smaller than Japan. (F)
Japan isn't smaller than Puerto Rico. (T)

9. 20 degrees C. is warmer than 50 degrees F. (T)
50 degrees F. is warmer than 20 degrees C. (F)
20 degrees C. isn't warmer than 50 degrees F. (F)
50 degrees F. isn't warmer than 20 degrees C. (T)

10. Two kilometers is longer than one mile. (T)
One mile is longer than two kilometers. (F)
Two kilometers isn't longer than one mile. (F)
One mile isn't longer than two kilometers. (T)

11. Television was invented more recently than the
telephone. (T)
The telephone was invented more recently than
television. (F)
Television wasn't invented more recently than the
telephone. (F)
The telephone wasn't invented more recently than
television. (T)

12. An orange has fewer calories than a banana. (T)
A banana has fewer calories than an orange. (F)
An orange doesn't have fewer calories than a
banana. (F)
A banana doesn't have fewer calories than an
orange. (T)

13. An alligator weighs less than a zebra. (T)
A zebra weighs less than an alligator. (F)
An alligator weighs less than a zebra. (F)
A zebra weighs less than an alligator. (T)

Comparative Trivia
Score Card

Player 1. Name:
Is the statement *true* ___ or *false* ___

Player 2. Name:
Is the statement *true* ___ or *false* ___

Player 3. Name:
Is the statement *true* ___ or *false* ___

Player 4. Name:
Is the statement *true* ___ or *false* ___

Player 5. Name:
Is the statement *true* ___ or *false* ___

Player 6. Name:
Is the statement *true* ___ or *false* ___

Player 7. Name:
Is the statement *true* ___ or *false* ___

Player 8. Name:
Is the statement *true* ___ or *false* ___

Player 9. Name:
Is the statement *true* ___ or *false* ___

Player 10. Name:
Is the statement *true* ___ or *false* ___

Player 11. Name:
Is the statement *true* ___ or *false* ___

Player 12. Name:
Is the statement *true* ___ or *false* ___

Player 13. Name:
Is the statement *true* ___ or *false* ___

Player 14. Name:
Is the statement *true* ___ or *false* ___

Player 15. Name:
Is the statement *true* ___ or *false* ___

Player 16. Name:
Is the statement *true* ___ or *false* ___

Player 17. Name:
Is the statement *true* ___ or *false* ___

Player 18. Name:
Is the statement *true* ___ or *false* ___

Player 19. Name:
Is the statement *true* ___ or *false* ___

Player 20. Name:
Is the statement *true* ___ or *false* ___

Player 21. Name:
Is the statement *true* ___ or *false* ___

Player 22. Name:
Is the statement *true* ___ or *false* ___

Party People

Language Focus

Comparisons of equality and inequality.

Summary of Game

Students identify the people at a party on the basis of descriptive clues.

Number of Players

Any number, divided into two or more teams of up to 11 members each.

Preparation by Teacher

Before Class
Make a copy of the **Party People** picture for each student. Make a copy of the **Clues** and cut them out.

In Class
1. Divide the class into two or more teams.
2. Give each student a copy of the **Party** picture and one slip of paper containing a **Clue**. Distribute **Clues** evenly among the members of a team.
3. Write the names of **Party** characters on the board, in two lists. The men are **John, Fred, Lou, Phil,** and **Bob.** The women are **Mildred, Marsha, Joan, Sally, Betty,** and **Jill.**

Directions to Students

1. There are 11 people at a party. Their names are on the board. Each of you has a sketch of these people and one or more sentences comparing them. Memorize your comparison.
2. Share your comparisons with your teammates.
3. Together, you'll identify the people and write their names in the boxes under their pictures.
4. The first team to identify everyone correctly wins.

For Small Classes
If your class is too small to divide into teams for this activity, give each student one or more slips of paper with a comparison on it and have the class work together to solve the mystery.

Phil is fatter than Lou.	Phil is shorter than Fred.
Joan is taller than Jill.	Bob is the shortest man at the party.
Mildred is older than Phil.	Jill is as tall as Mildred.
Marsha is taller than John.	Fred is shorter than Lou.
Phil is thinner than John.	Sally is the youngest person at the party.
Fred is younger than Mildred.	Betty seems happier than Joan.
Marsha is taller than Jill.	Sally has the curliest hair.
Joan is as tall as John.	Phil has less hair than Marsha.

Section: Comparisons

Jumping to Conclusions

Language Focus

Comparisons, gerunds.

Summary of Game

Students try to predict one another's responses to a survey.

Number of Players

Any number, in groups of 7 to 13.

Preparation by Teacher

Before Class
For each student in your class, make a copy of the **Survey Sheet** on the following page.

In Class
1. If you have a class of 14 or more students, divide it into groups of 7 to 13.
2. Distribute copies of the **Survey Sheet**, one to each student.
3. Discuss the examples of comparisons using gerunds given at the top of the **Survey Sheets** and also below. Have students brainstorm a list of additional gerunds; have a student write the list on the board as it is developed.
4. When giving directions to students, have them complete each step before you give instructions for the next step.

Directions to Students

1. At the top of the **Survey Sheet** you have been given, write your own statement comparing two activities and using two gerunds. Look at the examples.

   Swimming is more fun than riding a bicycle.
   Playing the guitar is harder to learn than skateboarding.
   Smoking is more dangerous to your health than eating two doughnuts every day.

2. Write the name of every student in your class/group in the spaces provided on your **Survey Sheet**.
3. Predict whether each student on your list will agree with your statement or disagree by writing an **A** for "agree" or a **D** for "disagree."
4. Circulate among your classmates, asking them whether they agree or disagree. Follow this model question: "Do you agree that swimming is more fun than riding a bicycle?"
5. Write an **A** if a classmate agrees with the statement or a **D** if he/she disagrees.
6. Total the number of correct predictions you made. The student with the largest number of correct predictions wins.

STATEMENT:_____

_____

SURVEY SHEET

JUMPING TO CONCLUSIONS

A = Agree
D = Disagree

NAMES OF STUDENTS	PREDICTED RESPONSE	ACTUAL RESPONSE

Have a Seat

Language Focus

Real conditions.

Summary of Game

Students figure out how to seat themselves in an arrangement determined by clues using real conditions.

Number of Players

Directions given are for 12 students. "Have a Seat" can be adapted for classes of 8 to 24. If there are fewer than 12 students, you can rewrite the clues or, to avoid rewriting, you and/or other volunteers can join in the game to come up with 12 players. For more than 12 students, you can rewrite, you can divide into two groups of 12 players with you and volunteers joining the additional students, or you can make up a similar set of at least 6 interrelated characters for another, different "Have a Seat" game.

Preparation by Teacher

Before Class
1. Make a copy of the **Clues**. Cut along the dotted lines so that you have one slip for each student.
2. Arrange 12 seats in 3 rows of 4 (see the **Solution**).
3. Put a red book under the second seat from the left in the middle row.

In Class
1. The students gather standing near the seats.
2. Point out rows 1, 2, and 3.
3. Give each student a **Clue** slip.

Directions to Students

Your slip tells you your name and a few bits of information about you and about where you should sit. The object of the game is to find your seat as quickly as possible. To do so, ask your classmates questions.

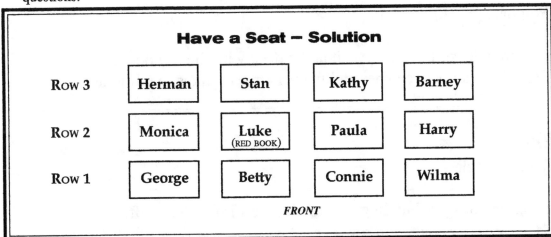

Have a Seat – Solution

Row 3	Herman	Stan	Kathy	Barney
Row 2	Monica	Luke (RED BOOK)	Paula	Harry
Row 1	George	Betty	Connie	Wilma

FRONT

Herman
(You're an architect.)

If Betty is married, sit directly in front of Connie. If not, sit in a corner seat.

Monica
(You have no brothers or sisters.)

If Harry is a father, sit in row two. If Wilma hates pizza, sit in row three.

George
(You're a chef.)

If Kathy is a gardener, sit in front of the only child. If not, sit behind the only child.

Stan
(You're a comic.)

If Paula can dance, sit to Barney's immediate right. If not, sit between the architect and Kathy.

Luke
(You hate pizza.)

If Connie doesn't like to fly, sit at the desk with the red book.
If she does, sit between her and the person who likes to tell jokes.

Betty
(You're single.)

If Herman designs buildings, sit to George's immediate left.
If George is a cook, sit in row one.

Kathy
(You grow roses.)

If Monica is sitting in row three, sit in row two. If she's in row two, sit in row three.

Paula
(You can't dance.)

If Barney doesn't have a cigar, sit two seats to Connie's right.
If he does, sit between the red book and the father.

Connie
(You don't like to fly.)

If Wilma hates pizza, sit behind her. If she doesn't, don't.

Barney
(You have a cigar.)

If Monica has a twin sister, sit at the seat with the red book.
If Stan isn't a teacher, sit in a corner seat two places behind the pizza lover.

Harry
(You have three children.)

If Paula is a ballet dancer, sit to George's left.
If she isn't, sit in an end seat of row two.

Wilma
(You like pizza.)

If Harry has only two children, sit behind Luke.
If he has more, sit next to Connie.

What If?

Language Focus

Present unreal conditions with the verb *to be.*

Summary of Game

Working in small teams, students imagine classmates as other things, like vegetables or flowers. Then they listen to the characterizations imagined by other teams and try to identify the classmates described.

Number of Players

Any number, divided into small working teams of 3 or 5 students.

Preparation by Teacher

Before Class

1. Write the name of each student in your class on a separate **Name** card, a 3x5 index card.
2. From the list on the **Answer** sheet, choose the same number of categories as there are students in the class. Write each category you've chosen on a separate **Category** index card. (Use cards of one color for students' names and cards of a different color for the categories to help ease distribution.)
3. Decide how many working teams you're going to have.
4. Make one copy each of the **Answer** and the **Characterization** sheets for each team.
5. Write a time limit on the board. About 2 minutes per student to be characterized is appropriate.

In Class

1. Divide the class into working teams.
2. Give each team as many **Name** cards and **Category** cards as there are students on the team. Also give each team an **Answer** sheet and a **Characterization** sheet.

Directions to Students

1. You and your teammates have cards with the names of members of the class and an equal number of cards with category headings. Match each class member with a category, and then think of a specific example of things in that category that fit that person. For example, you might characterize *Juanita* as a *building* and specifically as a *library.*
2. On the **Characterization** sheet, write your characterizations in unreal conditional sentences, adding your reasons for each characterization like this: "If X were a *building,* she would be a *library,* because she *likes to read.* "You will have _____ minutes to discuss and write your characterizations. (Point out the time limit on the board.)
3. As a team, read your characterizations to another team. Each of you should read one sentence. Be sure not to read students' names. Say "X" instead. On their **Answer** sheet, members of the other team will write the *specific examples* and *reasons* mentioned, next to the categories you mention. The other team then reads you their characterizations, and you fill out your **Answer** sheet.
4. Through discussion with your teammates, try to identify the person being characterized in each category. Write each person's name next to the matching category. (You should fill in the names of the people that your own team has characterized.)
5. If there are other teams and enough time, meet with another team and figure out who they are characterizing. Then, as a class, identify how each classmate was characterized. The team with the greatest number of correct matches wins.

"What If?" Characterizations

Example:

If X were a building, she would be a library, because she loves to read.

"What If?" Answers

Person	Category	Specifically	Reason
_____	building	_____	_____
_____	footwear	_____	_____
_____	plant	_____	_____
_____	furniture	_____	_____
_____	season	_____	_____
_____	room	_____	_____
_____	city	_____	_____
_____	time of day	_____	_____
_____	car	_____	_____
_____	movie star	_____	_____
_____	vegetable	_____	_____
_____	month	_____	_____
_____	color	_____	_____
_____	day of the week	_____	_____
_____	music	_____	_____
_____	musical instrument	_____	_____
_____	sport	_____	_____
_____	article of clothing	_____	_____
_____	fabric	_____	_____
_____	drink	_____	_____
_____	animal	_____	_____
_____	part of speech	_____	_____
_____	flower	_____	_____
_____	food	_____	_____
_____	Disney character	_____	_____

Hot Seat

Language Focus

Present (simple and continuous) unreal conditionals.

Summary of Game

In teams composed of a "hot seat" contestant and several panel members, panel members try to match the contestant's answers to hypothetical questions.

Number of Players

Any number, divided into teams of 4–5 students: 1 hot seat contestant and 3–4 panel members.

Preparation by Teacher

Before Class
1. Have ready large slips of paper or large index cards on which students will write their answers. Other members of the class should be able to read them.
2. Arrange seats in groups of 4 or 5. Panel members should not be able to see the hot seat contestant's answers.

In Class
1. Divide the class into teams, seated according to your arrangement.
2. Choose (or have team members choose) a hot seat contestant for each team. The other team members compose the panel.

Directions to Students

1. The teacher (or a student, if the teams could not be divided evenly) will read a **Question** with a conditional clause.
2. The hot-seaters will write their answers hidden from the members of their panels. The panel members write the answers that they think their hot seat contestant wrote.
3. When "time" is called (for example, 10 seconds), the hot-seaters will be asked to hold up their answers. Panel members are then asked to hold up their answers. The team receives one point for each match. At the end of the game, the team with the most points wins.

QUESTIONS

Hot Seat

1. If you were a famous actor, which one would you be?

2. If you were in your room right now listening to music, what kind of music would you be listening to?

3. If you were eating ice cream now, what flavor would you be eating?

4. If you were on vacation in Europe right now, which country would you be in?

5. If a stranger on the street asked for some money, how much would you give?

6. If you were a teacher, which subject would you teach?

7. If you were sad, which room of your house would you like to be in?

8. If you were married, how many children would you have?

9. If you were an animal, which animal would you be?

10. If you could live wherever you wanted, would you live on an island?

11. If you had to choose only one of the following, would you be extremely . . . rich, good-looking, intelligent, or strong?

12. If you had to choose only one subject to get an "A" in, which one would it be?

13. If you were stranded on a desert island, what is the one thing that you would want to have with you?

14. If all of your clothes had to be the same color, what color would they be?

15. If you had only one food to eat every day for a week, what food would it be?

_____

_____

_____

_____

_____

Section: Conditional Sentences   42

Conditional Chain Reaction

Language Focus

Real and unreal conditions.

Summary of Game

In a chain format, the conclusion of one conditional sentence is made the condition of a new one.

Number of Players

Any number.

Preparation by Teacher

In Class
1. Seat the students in a circle.
2. Choose one of the conditional clauses, real or unreal, from the lists below. Read the clause aloud or write it on the board.

Directions to Students

You will be given an *if* clause. Student A will make a conditional sentence by repeating the *if* clause and adding a conclusion. Student B will make a new sentence by changing A's conclusion into an *if* clause and adding a new conclusion. Here's an example:

Teacher: **If Fred took a trip ...**
A. If Fred took a trip, he would go to Paris.
B. If Fred went to Paris, he would climb the Eiffel Tower.
C. If Fred climbed the Eiffel Tower, he would get tired.

Suggestions

1. This can be done with a ball or beanbag. Once a student gives an *if* clause, they toss the ball to another student, who adds the conclusion.
2. An additional game element can be added by limiting the time each student has to give a correct conclusion. Use a timer to set a time limit, perhaps 10 seconds. If they cannot come up with an answer within the time limit, or if they make an error, they drop out of the round.
3. After a student gives a conclusion, the teacher can ask the other students if they want to challenge the sentence. If they challenge a correct sentence, they drop out. If they challenge an incorrect sentence, the student who made the error drops out. If no one challenges an incorrect answer, the teacher corrects the sentence, but the student who made the error stays in the round.
4. At some point in the game, tell the students to reverse the order of the *if* clause and the conclusion—for example, "Fred would go to Paris if he took a trip ."

Real Conditional Clauses
1. If Fred finds a wallet containing $200, ...
2. If a black cat crosses Fred's path, ...
3. If Fred enters a talent contest, ...
4. If Fred takes a trip to Hollywood, ...
5. If Fred gets a job at McDonald's, ...

Unreal Conditional Clauses
6. If Fred met aliens from outer space, ...
7. If Fred could make himself invisible, ...
8. If Fred could travel through time, ...
9. If a magician changed Fred into a dog, ...
10. If Fred were telepathic, ...

43

Fractured Sentences

Language Focus

Verbs and expressions that are followed by gerunds and infinitives.

Summary of Game

Working in teams, students compose as many sentences as possible from given words and punctuation.

Number of Players

Any number, divided into teams of 2–8 students, depending on class size.

Preparation by Teacher

Before Class

1. Determine how many teams you need to have.
2. From the following pages, duplicate one complete set of the playing cards with words and punctuation marks for each team.
3. Cut out the cards. You'll have 108 for each team. Mix up the cards in each set. Keep the sets separate, if you have more than one.

In Class

Each team has a pile of small cards with words and punctuation marks on them. The object is to work with the other students on your team to arrange cards forming as many sentences as you can in 10 minutes using each card only once. The team with the highest score wins. Scoring is as follows:

2 points for each grammatically correct sentence with a gerund or infinitive
1 point for each grammatically correct sentence without a gerund or infinitive

MY	PAULA'S	NOT	THE
AUNT	SHE	WE	TEAM
ENJOY	ARE	BUYING	DOES
SEVERAL	SAM'S	HIM	WATCHING
BOYS	IT	US	BASEBALL
DISCUSSED	IS	HAVE	ON
THEIR	DOG	NEW	TV
HE	SISTER	EQUIPMENT	LIKE
WILL	HAS	FOR	PLANNING

45   *Section: Gerunds and Infinitives*

Playing Cards for Fractured Sentences

TO	AT	TAKE	QUIT
INVITE	THE	OUR	SMOKING
TO	CAT	UMBRELLA	SOON
HIS	LAST	ON	YOU
PARTY	NIGHT	THE	REMIND
NEXT	FRIEND	AIRPLANE	ME
SATURDAY	ADVISED	I	TO
KEPT	NOT	PROMISE	RETURN
BARKING	TO	TO	MY

LIBRARY	BETWEEN	MARCO	**?**
USE	MONEY	CREDIT CARD	**?**
BOOK	TAKE	USING	**?**
WOULD	SPENDING	YOU	**.**
TRAVELING	FLIGHTS	MIND	**.**
BUS	BUY	OPENING	**.**
ACROSS	TAKING	THE	**.**
WE	SHIRTS	WINDOW	**.**
WALKING	TO	**?**	**.**

Asking Favors

Language Focus

Formulas for asking favors, such as:

"Would you mind ...?"
"Can you ...?"
"Would you be free to ...?"
"Could you ...?"
"Would you be willing to ...?"

Summary of Game

Students ask others for help with planned activities, and fill in appointment calendars.

Number of Players

Any number.

Preparation by Teacher

Before Class
Make a copy of the **Appointment Calendar** for each student.

In Class
Hand out copies of the **Appointment Calendar**. Write the formulas for polite requests on the board.

Directions to Students

1. You each have an **Appointment Calendar** for next week. Each day is divided into morning, afternoon, and evening.
2. Fill in five of the squares with activities you plan to do and need help with—for example:

   "Wash my car."
   "Do my math homework."
   "Pick up my brother after school."

3. You have two goals:
   a. To find classmates who are free to help you with your five planned activities. When you ask them for their help, use one of the polite expressions on the board. If they agree, have them sign their names in the squares under the activities. You may have no more than two signatures from the same person.
   b. To fill in the rest of your calendar with activities with which your classmates have asked you for help.

Note
For smaller classes, the winner is the student with the most activities on his or her **Appointment Calendar**. For larger classes, the winner is the first student to fill in his or her **Calendar** with activities.

Evening	Afternoon	Morning	
			Sunday
			Monday
			Tuesday
			Wednesday
			Thursday
			Friday
			Saturday

The Genuine "Asking Favors" Appointment Calendar

Section: Gerunds and Infinitives

Canned Bingo

Language Focus

Can and *can't* used for ability.

Summary of Game

Students circulate, asking about the abilities of other students in order to fill in a **Bingo Card**.

Number of Players

Any number.

Preparation by Teacher

Before Class
Make a copy of one of the **Bingo Cards** for each student.

In Class
Distribute the copies.

Directions to Students

1. You each have a **Bingo Card**.
2. Walk around the classroom and ask classmates if they can do the things mentioned on the **Bingo Card**. Ask yes/no questions using *can*—for example:

   "Can you fly an airplane?"

3. For boxes with *can,* find a classmate who answers "yes." Write that person's name in the appropriate box.
4. For boxes with *can't,* find a classmate who answers "no." Write that person's name in the appropriate box.
5. The first student to have five names in a row, vertically, horizontally, or diagonally, wins.

Can ride a skateboard	Can wiggle his/her ears	Can't speak 3 languages	Can play a stringed instrument	Can ice skate
Can bake a cake	Can't say a tongue twister	Can ride a horse	Can tell a joke in English	Can't swim
Can't eat with chopsticks	Can't play golf	Can spell the teacher's last name	Can't hold his/her breath for 45 seconds	Can hop backwards on one foot
Can stand on his/her head	Can make an origami bird	Can't spell the capital of Thailand	Can't name 3 countries in South America	Can play chess
Can't play pool	Can run 100 meters in 15 seconds	Can't name 5 states in the U.S. Midwest	Can name the last 3 presidents of the U.S.A.	Can cook homemade lasagne

Canned Bingo!

Section: Modals

Can't play checkers	Can eat with chopsticks	Can't name the last 3 presidents of the U.S.A.	Can swim	Can dive off a high board
Can't whistle the Happy Birthday song	Can't cook homemade lasagne	Can spell the teacher's first name	Can spell the capital of Thailand	Can name 4 states in the U.S. South
Can say a tongue twister	Can play golf	Can't wiggle his/her ears	Can't bake a cake	Can't stand on his/her head
Can't play a wind instrument	Can't tell a joke in English	Can't ski	Can't make an origami bird	Can't ride a snowboard
Can play poker	Can't ride a horse	Can name 3 countries in Africa	Can hold his/her breath for 45 seconds	Can speak 3 languages

Canned Bingo!

Sharing Should

Language Focus

Should and *shouldn't* used for obligation and prohibition.

Summary of Game

Students circulate, asking for classmates' opinions on what people should and shouldn't do, and fill in a **Survey** with the results..

Number of Players

Any number.

Preparation by Teacher

Before Class
Make a copy of the **Survey** for each student.

In Class
Distribute the copies.

Directions to Students

Using the **Survey** you've been given, circulate and ask yes/no questions with *should*—for example:

"Should all of the countries in the world belong to the United Nations?"

Notes
You might want to set a time limit (for example, 20 minutes) and also to limit the number of times a student can use the same classmate's name.

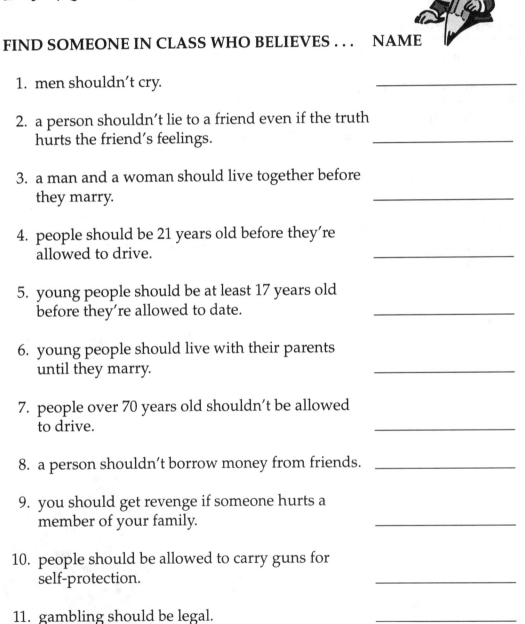

SURVEY

FIND SOMEONE IN CLASS WHO BELIEVES . . . NAME

1. men shouldn't cry. _____

2. a person shouldn't lie to a friend even if the truth
   hurts the friend's feelings. _____

3. a man and a woman should live together before
   they marry. _____

4. people should be 21 years old before they're
   allowed to drive. _____

5. young people should be at least 17 years old
   before they're allowed to date. _____

6. young people should live with their parents
   until they marry. _____

7. people over 70 years old shouldn't be allowed
   to drive. _____

8. a person shouldn't borrow money from friends. _____

9. you should get revenge if someone hurts a
   member of your family. _____

10. people should be allowed to carry guns for
    self-protection. _____

11. gambling should be legal. _____

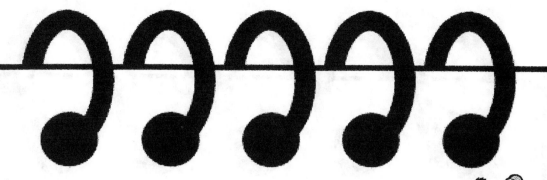

12. a woman should keep her family name when she marries.

_____

13. a man should be present when his wife gives birth.

_____

14. people shouldn't eat meat.

_____

15. mothers of young children shouldn't work outside the home.

_____

16. teenaged boys and girls should go to separate schools.

_____

17. you should tell the teacher if your friend is cheating on a test.

_____

18. you should let your friend copy your homework if your friend needs to.

_____

19. people who are dying shouldn't be free to take their own lives with the help of a doctor.

_____

20. teens shouldn't have their own telephones.

_____

21. students should be allowed to choose their own courses in high school.

_____

22. schools should have a dress code.

_____

23. a nation's government should be allowed to make laws limiting the number of children a couple may have.

_____

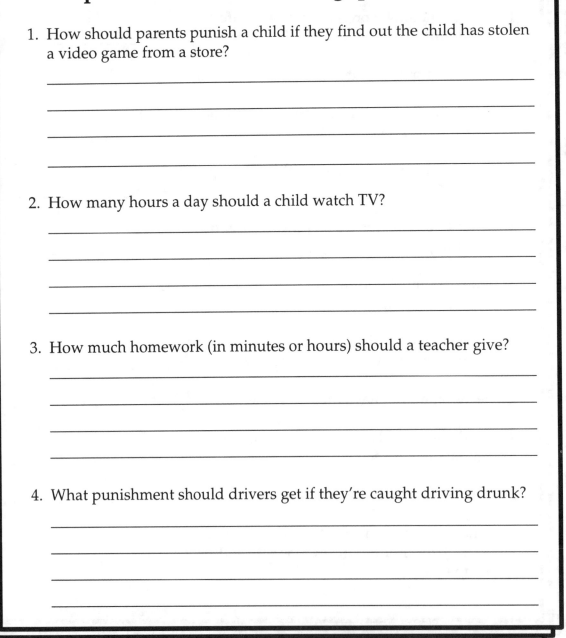

Survey at least four other students to get their opinions on the following questions:

1. How should parents punish a child if they find out the child has stolen a video game from a store?

   _____

   _____

   _____

   _____

2. How many hours a day should a child watch TV?

   _____

   _____

   _____

   _____

3. How much homework (in minutes or hours) should a teacher give?

   _____

   _____

   _____

   _____

4. What punishment should drivers get if they're caught driving drunk?

   _____

   _____

   _____

   _____

The Great Modal Race

Language Focus

Prediction
Might, might not, will probably, probably won't, may, may not, am definitely going to, and *am definitely not going to.*

Obligation
Must, must not, have to, don't have to, have got to, don't need to.

Summary of Game

Students, working in teams, construct sentences using modals of prediction and obligation. For each correct sentence, they extend a line indicating their race from city to city across a map.

Number of Players

Any number up to 40.

Preparation by Teacher

Before Class
1. Make two copies of the **Sentence Fragments** sheet. Cut along the lines so that you have two separate sets of 30 slips each.
2. Make two copies each of the **Obligation Tickets** and **Prediction Tickets**, one of each for each team. You may cut the tickets apart, or let the students drop pebble or coin markers onto the sheets and use the modals on which the markers land. The directions below assume that the tickets are cut apart.

In Class
1. Divide the class into two teams.
2. Give each team a map.

Directions to Students

1. Each team has a map on which 20 locations are marked. Your trip will be a race from the start to the finish.
2. Two of you from each team will stand up and take a slip of paper with two sets of sentence fragments on it. One of you will take a **Prediction Ticket**; the other will take an **Obligation Ticket**.
3. The two players from each team will make up sentences using the fragments and the modals on the tickets. They have about 20 seconds to discuss their sentences together before saying them to the class. For example, the fragments might be *go to the movies/my friend Maria* and *lots of money/ because*. The tickets might be *will probably* and *need to*. Correct sentences might be "I'll probably go to the movies with my friend Maria" and "You're going to need to bring lots of money, because Maria will want to go out for dinner after the movie."

   If the class agrees that the players' sentences are correct, one of the players can draw a line on the map moving their team ahead in the race. Whenever a team gets one set of correct sentences, one more pair of players from that team gets a turn and a chance to move ahead; after a team has had two turns, they have to let the other team have a turn. If the first pair of players does not make correct sentences, they lose their turn to the other team.
4. The first team to reach the finish line after getting 20 correct sentences wins The Great Modal Race.

Sentence Fragments for The Great Modal Race

1. Student A: buy a Honda / a lot of power Student B: to drive carefully / children	16. Student A: sick / healthy Student B: health insurance / costs a lot
2. Student A: a fine French restaurant Student B: mother-in-law / hungry	17. Student A: catch a bus / Orlando Student B: pickpocket / broke
3. Student A: climb Pike's Peak / car Student B: climbing gear / safety	18. Student A: plant tomatoes / spring Student B: pick / ripe
4. Student A: course in zoology / Lyons Student B: lab work / monster textbook	19. Student A: leave my car / parking lot Student B: lock / stereo
5. Student A: skiing at night / no wind Student B: pay full price / stars / beautiful	20. Student A: get pregnant / want to Student B: Dr. Chang / care
6. Student A: win the marathon / April Student B: training / eating	21. Student A: write to Aunt Sally / invite Student B: ask / Uncle Karl / ill
7. Student A: arrange / flowers Student B: help / party	22. Student A: dishes / dishwasher Student B: break / expensive
8. Student A: roast a pig / party Student B: burn / well done / raw	23. Student A: surf / Internet Student B: homework / big exam
9. Student A: Italian / Florence Student B: waste / shopping	24. Student A: invite / Paul and Rosa Student B: vacuum / filthy
10. Student A: haircut / Joe the Barber Student B: forty bucks / Magic Mirror	25. Student A: trip / seashore Student B: map / lost
11. Student A: lobsters and steamed clams Student B: try / afraid	26. Student A: arrest / burglar Student B: insurance / gone
12. Student A: fight / World Heavyweight Student B: enjoy / violence	27. Student A: pet hamster / Harry Student B: cat / disappear
13. Student A: English 601 / Shakespeare Student B: understand the language	28. Student A: fast / late at night Student B: ticket / license
14. Student A: enjoy a rich dessert Student B: loose weight / tomorrow	29. Student A: new bathroom / colors Student B: wallpaper / expensive
15. Student A: paint a picture / grandson Student B: show / angry	30. Student A: Delta / LA / Atlanta Student B: late / miss

The Great Modal Race Prediction Tickets

using *might, might not, will probably, probably won't, may, may not,*
am definitely going to, and *am definitely not going to*

might	may	might	will probably
will probably	am definitely not going to	may not	are definitely not going to
may not	probably won't	are definitely going to	may
probably won't	am definitely not going to	might not	might
am definitely not going to	may not	probably won't	are definitely going to
may	might not	might	may not
might not	am definitely going to	may	will probably
am definitely going to	might not	will probably	probably won't
will probably	may	are definitely not going to	might not

Section: Modals

The Great Modal Race Obligation Tickets

using *must, must not, have to, don't have to,*
have got to, need to, and *don't need to*

must	need to	have to	have got to
don't have to	have to	must	don't need to
have to	mustn't	don't have to	must
have got to	need to	must not	do not have to
must	have got to	mustn't	have to
don't have to	have to	have got to	must
have got to	doesn't have to	need to	have got to
need to	mustn't	have to	mustn't
mustn't	must	don't have to	need to

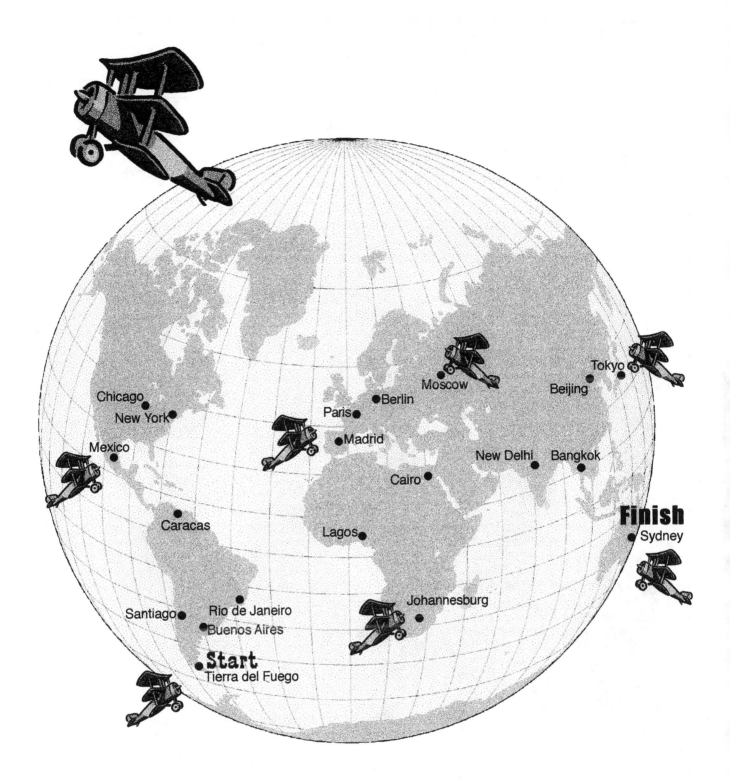

The Great Modal Race
Around The World

The Great Modal Race
Around North America

Job Skills

Language Focus

Necessity: Have to, have got to, and *need to.*

Summary of Game

Students figure out classmates' assumed occupations by asking questions about qualifications and skills necessary for each job.

Number of Players

4–22.

Preparation by Teacher

Before Class
1. Make a copy of the **Occupations** sheet. Cut out the 22 separate slips.
2. Make a copy of the **Skills** sheet for each student.

In Class
1. Give one **Occupation** slip to each student. Tell students not to let anyone else know what is written on their slips.
2. Give each student a copy of the **Skills** sheet.

Directions to Students

1. Each of you has been assigned one of the **Occupations** listed on the **Skills** sheet. Your task is to discover which classmate has which occupation by asking questions about the qualifications and skills necessary for that job.
2. Typical questions might be:

    "Do you have to have strong calf muscles for your job?"
    "Do you need to be athletic?"
    "Do you have to read music for your profession?"
    "Have you got to change your appearance for your job?"
    "To be safe, do you need to disguise yourself in your job?"

3. You must not ask directly, "Are you a telephone operator?" or "Are you a basketball coach?"
4. When time is called, the student who has correctly identified the professions of the largest number of classmates wins.

Note
You also may want to introduce the longer phrase "Is it necessary to ..." The modal *must* is grammatically correct when used in this context—for example, "Must I wear a tie in the office?" However, it is not current colloquial American usage. You might want to introduce *must* for necessity, but tell the students that it is not normally used and will probably sound "stuffy" to most Americans.

airline pilot	plastic surgeon
ballet dancer	wrestler
aerobics instructor	trumpet player
driving instructor	basketball coach
animal trainer	truck driver
kindergarten teacher	funeral director
auto mechanic	nurse
ice cream taste tester	landscape architect
race car driver	actor
telephone operator	juggler
novelist	pastry chef
bank robber	caterer

SKILLS

OCCUPATION	NAME
airline pilot	_____
ballet dancer	_____
aerobics instructor	_____
driving instructor	_____
animal trainer	_____
kindergarten teacher	_____
auto mechanic	_____
ice cream taste tester	_____
race car driver	_____
telephone operator	_____
novelist	_____
bank robber	_____
plastic surgeon	_____
wrestler	_____
trumpet player	_____
basketball coach	_____
truck driver	_____
funeral director	_____
nurse	_____
landscape architect	_____
actor	_____
juggler	_____
pastry chef	_____
caterer	_____

Shopping List

Language Focus

Count and non-count nouns.

Summary of Game

Students have to remember all the items mentioned by the other students in a circle, and correctly use *a few* and *a little*.

Number of Players

5 or more.

Preparation by Teacher

Before Class
1. Students will have to know each other's names. If they aren't well acquainted, you might want to make name tags to help maintain the pace of the game.
2. The class will be divided into two groups: seated players and standing reserves. While the two groups don't have to be equal in number, there should be an odd number of seated players. Arrange chairs for the seated players, in a circle if possible.

In Class
1. Arrange players and reserves.
2. Remind students to listen to each other very carefully.

Directions to Students

1. The first student in the circle will complete the sentence "I went to the supermarket and bought *a few* ..." with a count noun like *apples*.
2. The second student must repeat the first student's sentence and add a *non*-count noun preceded by *a little*, like "I went to the supermarket and bought *a few* apples and *a little* milk."
3. The third student repeats and adds a count noun: "I went to the supermarket and bought *a few* apples, *a little* milk, and *a few* cassette tapes." The game continues around the circle in this way.
4. Students may not write during this game.
5. If a student cannot remember all the preceding items or uses *a little* or *a few* incorrectly, they are out of the circle and must name one of the students standing in reserve to take over their position. The eliminated student joins the reserve group. Since a member of the reserve group may become a player at any time, all of the reserves should pay close attention to the game.

Note
You may want to try this game allowing the students to choose any nouns they want—in other words, not alternating count and non-count automatically. This makes it easier in one way, because they can choose any noun, but more difficult in another because they can't depend on the predictable alternation.

Variations

1. This same game can be used to practice irregular plural noun forms: "I went to the zoo and saw not one goose but several geese, not one child but several children, and not one fish but several fish." You and the students may wish to brainstorm a list of creatures one might see at the zoo and put it on the board before playing the game. That way the players will have both regular and irregular nouns to work with, adding to the fun and the challenge.

2. You can also practice collective nouns: "I went to the zoo and saw a flock of geese, a pride of lions, and a crowd of children."

Noun Clues Crossword

Language Focus

Object noun clauses, and words that can introduce them.

Summary of Game

Students put clues about a thief into noun clauses and use the first words of the clauses to solve a crossword puzzle—and to figure out the identity of the thief.

Number of Players

Ideally, 11 students. With classes of different sizes, it may be necessary to give some students more than one clue or to have more than one student work with a clue.

Preparation by Teacher

Before Class
1. Make copies of the **Report Sheet** and the blank **Crossword** for each student.
2. Make a single copy of the **Clues**.
3. Cut out the **Clues** so you have 11 slips.

In Class
Give each student a **Report Sheet**, a **Crossword**, and one **Clue**.

Directions to Students

1. You have been given **Clues** about a fictional crime, a **Report Sheet**, and a blank **Crossword** puzzle to help you figure out who committed the crime. Your first task is to find out what each of your classmates knows about the crime.
2. Circulate. Ask, "What do you know about the thief?" On the appropriate lines of your **Report Sheet**, write down what each classmate knows as an indirect statement. For example, one student might have as a **Clue,** "The thief is 38 years old." That student's answer to "What do you know about the thief?" would be, "I know that the thief is 38 years old." Then, for that student, you would write on the **Report Sheet** "(Student's name) knows how old the thief is."
3. Your second task is to fill in the **Crossword**. For each response to the question, the first word(s) after "knows"—"how old," in the example—will fit in the appropriate place there. *Note:* The number and letter for each **Clue** refer to the **Crossword**. For instance, D10 means 10 *down,* and A5 means 5 *across.*
4. Your third task is to take the circled letters in the **Crossword** and rearrange them to name the thief.
5. The first person who can fill in the blanks in the **Solution** is the winner.

THE SOLUTION to the Noun Clues Mystery

The thief is _the mechanic_ who used to work at the shop down the street.

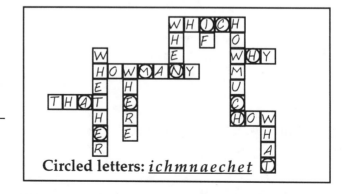

Circled letters: *ichmnaechet* *t*

OFFICIAL REPORT SHEET

Noun Clues Crossword

Crossword Square	Player's Name	Clues
Across		
A1	knows	
A5	knows	
A6	knows	
A8	knows	
A9	knows	
Down		
D1	knows	
D2	knows	
D3	knows	
D4	knows	
D7	knows	
D10	knows	

Noun Clues Crossword Puzzle

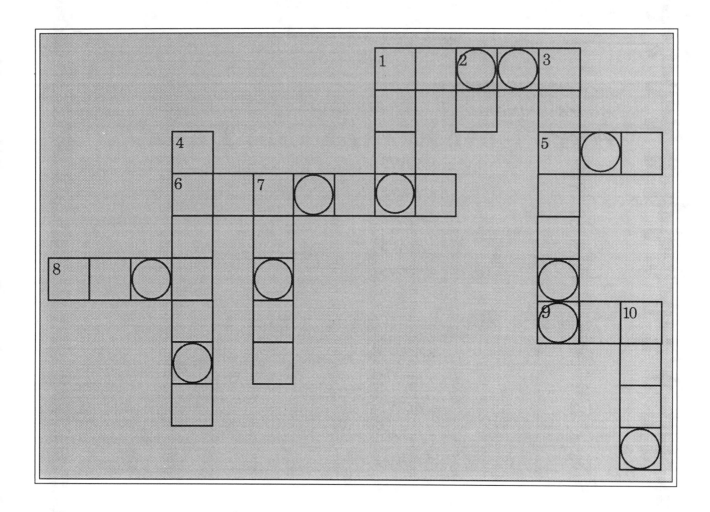

THE SOLUTION TO THE NOUN CLUES MYSTERY

The thief is _____ who used to work at the shop down the street.

10d. The thief stole jewelry.

5a. The thief chose this house to rob because there was an open window.

7d. The thief hid the stolen goods in the trunk of the car.

6a. There was only one thief.

4d. The thief didn't steal the television.

1a. The thief robbed the blue house.

9a. The thief entered the house through the window.

8a. The thief is a woman.

1d. The thief entered the house at 11 p.m.

2d. The thief carried a gun.

3d. The thief got $5000 for the stolen goods.

71   *Section: Noun Clauses*

Amazing Survey

Language Focus

Present and past participles used as adjectives. *Note:* This activity is most effective for students who are familiar with the use of gerunds and adjective clauses.

Summary of Game

Students fill in the blanks in a survey by selecting participles from a list and adding related gerund phrases or adjective clauses. Then they use the completed survey to question classmates.

Number of Players

Any number.

Preparation by Teacher

Before Class
Make a copy of the **Page of Examples and Participles** and the **Survey** for each student.

In Class
Have students complete the **Survey**. You can check the students' accuracy by either (1) collecting the completed forms and conducting the **Survey** the following day or (2) checking the students' work as they complete the forms.

Directions to Students

1. Each of you has a page giving 3 examples and a list of participles (marked **A**), and a **Survey**.
2. Read the 3 examples and the list of participles, and be sure you understand them.
3. Choosing participles from list **A** (such as *surprised* or *amazing*), fill in the blanks in your **Survey**. For each question, in blank (a) write the participle you've chosen.
5. Invent and write, in the blanks marked (b) and (c), two phrases or clauses listing things that can be described by the participle. See the examples.
6. After you've filled in the blanks on your **Survey**, ask the other students in your class the questions. Count the number of people who choose (b) or (c), and write the numbers where it says **Results**. When you've completed your survey, share the results with the class.

     72

Amazing Survey
Examples
of Questions

EXAMPLE #1: What do you think is more _____*embarrassing*_____ :
                                                    (a)

_____*smiling at someone who doesn't smile back*_____ or
                          (b)

_____*walking into the wrong rest-room*_____ ?
                     (c)

EXAMPLE #1: Who do you think is more _____*boring*_____ :
                                                 (a)

_____*someone who shows you pictures of their family*_____ or
                              (b)

_____*someone who tells you a story you've already heard*_____ ?
                                (c)

EXAMPLE #1: Who do you think is more _____*bored*_____ :
                                                (a)

_____*a child who can't go outside to play on a rainy Saturday*_____ or
                                  (b)

_____*a husband who is shopping for clothes with his wife*_____ ?
                               (c)

List of Participles A

SURPRISED	EMBARRASSED	CHALLENGING
AMAZING	ANNOYING	AMUSED
EXCITING	TIRED	CONFUSED
CONFUSING	SATISFIED	INSULTING
FRIGHTENED	DISAPPOINTED	SHOCKED
INTERESTING	REWARDING	FRIGHTENING

The Amazing Survey

1. What do you think is more _____:
                                        (a)

_____ or
                (b)

_____ ?
                (c)

RESULTS: b: _____ c: _____

2. What do you think is more _____:
                                        (a)

_____ or
                (b)

_____ ?
                (c)

RESULTS: b: _____ c: _____

3. What do you think is more _____:
                                        (a)

_____ or
                (b)

_____ ?
                (c)

RESULTS: b: _____ c: _____

The Amazing Survey, cont.

4. Who do you think is more _____:
   (a)

_____ or
   (b)

_____ ?
   (c)

RESULTS: b: _____ c: _____

5. Who do you think is more _____:
   (a)

_____ or
   (b)

_____ ?
   (c)

RESULTS: b: _____ c: _____

6. Who do you think is more _____:
   (a)

_____ or
   (b)

_____ ?
   (c)

RESULTS: b: _____ c: _____

Crowded Crossword

Language Focus

Present and past participles used as adjectives.

Summary of Game

Students complete clues with participles used as adjectives. Then they use the participles to solve a crossword puzzle.

Number of Players

6–22, working (a) as individuals or (b) in two teams, for larger classes.

Preparation by Teacher

Before Class
1. Decide whether you're going to have the students work individually or in teams.
2. Make a copy of the blank **Crowded Crossword** puzzle for each student or each team.
3. Make one copy of the **Clues** for the class or for each team.
4. If you plan to work with teams, arrange each group's chairs in a circle.

In Class
1. *Individual method:* Give each student a copy of the blank **Crowded Crossword** puzzle and 1 to 4 **Clues**, depending on the size of the class.
2. *Team method:* Divide the class into two groups. Give each team one copy of the **Crowded Crossword** puzzle. Then give one set of **Clues** to each group, as evenly distributed as possible among the members of the group.

Directions to Students

1. *Individual method:* Each of you has one or more **Clues** to the **Crowded Crossword** puzzle. Work together to fill in the puzzle. I will time you. See how fast you can finish.
2. *Team method:* Each of you has one or more **Clues** to the **Crowded Crossword** puzzle. Work together to fill in the blanks in the **Clues** and solve the puzzle before the other group does.

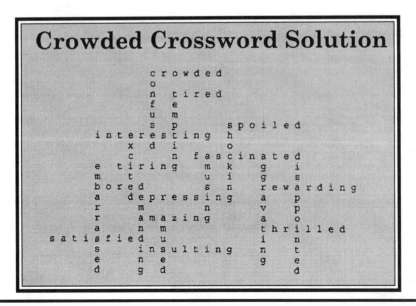

Crowded Crossword Puzzle

Crowded Crossword Clues—Across

A1. The elevator was too _____, so I waited for the next one.

A2. Bill is very _____ today because he didn't get much sleep last night.

A3. Their young son is _____. They give him everything he wants.

A4. We never miss our ESL class because it is so _____.

A6. The students had never seen a glass blower at work. They were _____ as they watched him make a vase.

A11. Moving the furniture was a very _____ job because it required a lot of strength and energy.

A12. Nancy was so _____ by the movie that she walked out before it was over.

A14. Dr. Jones finds being a physician a _____ profession. In addition to the satisfaction she receives from helping people, she earns a good salary.

A15. It is _____ to step on a scale after two weeks of dieting and find that you have lost only one pound.

A16. The audience found David Copperfield's magic trick _____. They were astonished and could not figure out how he had done it.

A18. The skier was _____ to win a gold medal at the Olympics. It was the most exciting day of her life.

A19. The store manager believes that customers who are _____ with the service and quality of the merchandise will continue to shop in his store.

A20. Barbara was offended by her sister's _____ comment about her weight.

D1. I was _____ after the math teacher explained the problem. I didn't understand it at all.

D2. Despite the _____ offer of a higher salary at the competitor's company, Angela decided to stay in her present position.

D3. The movie was _____ to many people in the audience who had not realized that it contained so much sex and violence.

D5. The child was _____ when his parents took him to the amusement park.

D7. Everyone always laughs at Uncle Bob's _____ stories.

D8. Because Betty likes to drive fast, she finds it _____ to be behind someone who drives 10 mph under the speed limit.

D9. Tyler expected to get an A on his grammar test. He was _____ because he got only a C.

D10. John was _____ when he realized that he didn't have enough money to pay the bill.

D13. This course is very _____. It requires a lot of reading, homework, several papers, and an oral report.

D17. Although Uncle Bob's anecdotes are usually funny, I was not _____ when he told an embarrassing story about me.

Spitting Image

Language Focus

Possessive nouns; vocabulary for parts of the body.

Summary of Game

Students exchange descriptions of what physical traits a baby inherited from its mother and its father to come up with a composite drawing of the child.

Number of Players

Any number.

Preparation by Teacher

Before Class

1. Copy **Descriptions** and cut them out. (For larger classes, determine how many groups you'll have, and make a copy of **Descriptions** for each group. If necessary, omit some **Descriptions**.)
2. Make one copy of the **Family Picture** (the one with the baby's face omitted) for each student.

Directions to Students

1. Mr. and Mrs. Luke Alyke are proud parents. Like most children, their child resembles the father in some ways and the mother in others. You haven't seen the child, but from the **Descriptions** you'll hear, you should be able to draw an accurate picture.
2. You each have one **Description**. Memorize it, and draw the body part as described on the **Family Picture**.
3. Circulate among your classmates sharing **Descriptions**.
4. Sketch the baby's features according to the **Description** you hear.
5. When you have a complete picture of the child, compare it with the pictures drawn by other students and with the **Official Family Portrait** that your teacher has.

FAMILY PICTURE

Spitting Image

OFFICIAL FAMILY PORTRAIT

The child has the father's freckles.

The child has the mother's nose.

The child has the father's mouth.

The child has the father's ears.

The child has the mother's hair.

The child has the mother's eyebrows.

The child has the mother's chin.

The child has the father's eyes.

The child has the father's shoulders.

The child has the mother's neck.

 Section: Possessive Nouns

Interactive Prefix Survey

Language Focus

Prefixes, yes/no questions.

Summary of Game

Students complete a survey by asking one another questions, each of which contains a word with a common prefix.

Number of Players

Any number.

Preparation by Teacher

Before Class
Make a copy of the **Survey** for each student.

In Class
Distribute the copies and announce a time limit.

Directions to Students

1. Circulate among your classmates asking yes/no questions based on the **Survey**. Survey as many classmates as possible, and get the signatures of those who can answer "yes" to your questions.
2. The winner is the student with the highest score when time is called. The score is the **total** number of signatures added to the number of **different** signatures (i.e., from different people).

The Interactive Prefix Survey

Get the signature of someone who . . .   SIGNATURES

is in favor of prenuptial agreements.   _____

disapproves of teachers wearing jeans.   _____

prefers semisweet chocolate to milk chocolate.   _____

would take an interplanetary trip if it were possible.   _____

can name a subtitled movie he or she has seen.   _____

can name a fictional superhero.   _____

has seen the reentry of a space shuttle.   _____

overslept one time last week.   _____

feels uncomfortable in hot weather.   _____

disagrees with his/her parents (or children) about curfew.   _____

knows someone who is self-employed.   _____

participates in an extracurricular activity.   _____

And of someone whose . . .

name is often mispronounced by native speakers of English.   _____

mother is bilingual.   _____

father is a nonsmoker.   _____

NUMBER OF SIGNATURES: _____

+ NUMBER OF DIFFERENT SIGNATURES: _____

= TOTAL SCORE: _____

Tiny Town, USA

Language Focus

Prepositional phrases of location.

Summary of Game

By sharing clues to locations, students identify the buildings on a drawing of a town.

Number of Players

7–13. (More can play if they are divided into groups.)

Preparation by Teacher

Before Class
1. Make a copy of the **Tiny Town** aerial view (map) for each student.
2. Make a copy of **Clues** for each group. Cut out the clues, so you have 13 slips for each group.

In Class
1. Give a copy of **Tiny Town** and a **Clue** to each student.
2. Have the students memorize the **Clues** and put the slips of paper away.

Directions to Students

1. You have the aerial view of **Tiny Town.** The shaded areas are buildings, but you can't identify the buildings from where you are without help.
2. Circulate among your classmates and share the **Clues** you have learned.
3. Your goal is to identify all the buildings in **Tiny Town**. Write the names on the buildings when you have identified them.

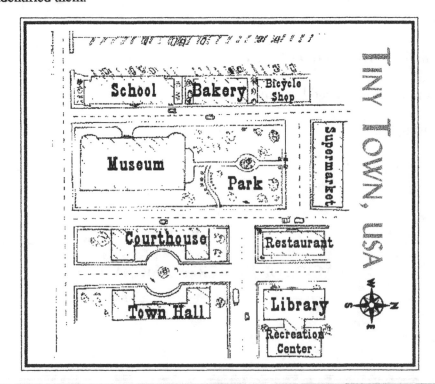

TINY TOWN, USA

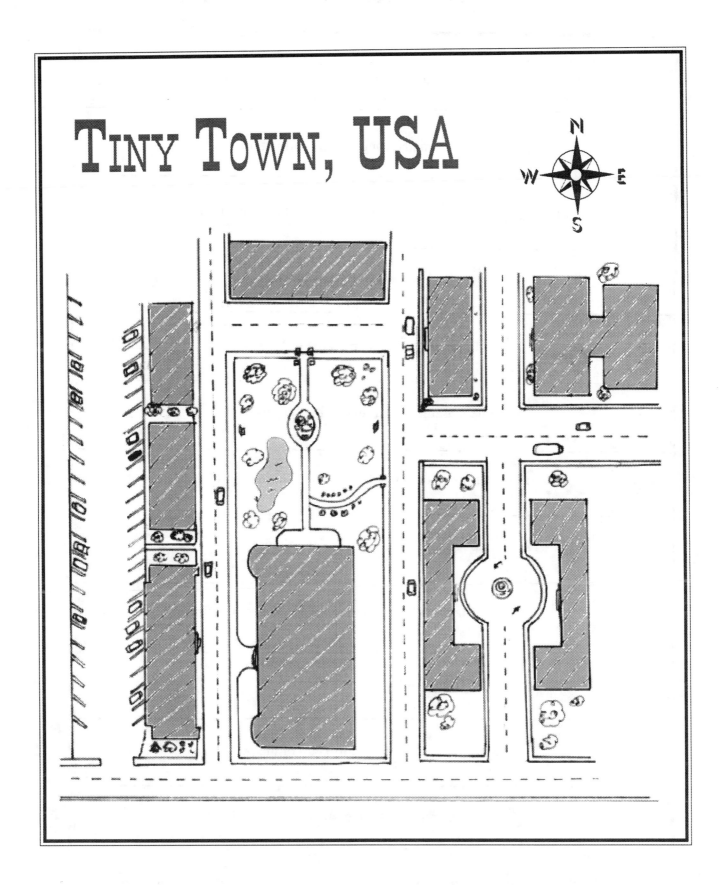

Section: Prepositions

The museum is located in the park.

The bakery stands alongside the parking lot.

The bakery is situated between the school and the bicycle shop.

The school is across from the museum.

The library is located behind the restaurant.

The museum is surrounded by the park.

The courthouse is situated in front of the town hall.

The restaurant is next to the courthouse.

The museum stands between the school and the courthouse.

The town hall is on the traffic circle.

The supermarket is at the north end of the park.

The supermarket faces the entrance to the park.

The library is beside the recreation center, and there is a connection between them.

Line Up

Language Focus

Information questions.

Summary of Game

Students line up as quickly as possible according to a series of instructions.

Number of Players

Any number.

Preparation by Teacher

In Class
Have students line up according to as many of the criteria below as you choose. (When the criterion is alphabetical, use the English alphabet.) Time them with a stopwatch or a watch with a second hand, as they try to beat their own record for how fast they can form a correct line.

Directions to Students

Line up as quickly as possible:

1. by age
2. alphabetically by your mother's first name (or her family name)
3. by the birthdate of your father
4. by the birthdate of your mother
5. alphabetically by the town or city you're from (If you're from the same city as another student, use the street name.)
6. by the amount of money you have in your pocket
7. by the house number of your current address
8. by the last two digits of your present telephone number
9. by the date of the last time you took a trip
10. by the time you got up this morning (or went to bed last night)
11. by the number of people who are in your family, including living grandparents, brothers and sisters, children, and grandchildren
12. alphabetically by the sport you enjoy playing the most
13. alphabetically by the name of your favorite food
14. by the number you choose between 1 and 500
15. by the number of people who could crowd into your classroom

Counter Questions

Language Focus

Yes/no questions.

Summary of Game

The students are divided into two teams, and each team makes up the details of an event. Then teams ask yes/no questions to try to discover the characters and circumstances in the event made up by the other team.

Number of Players

Any number.

Preparation by Teacher

1. Divide the class into two teams.
2. Duplicate one of the 5 **Counter Questions Worksheets**. You can give the teams the same or different worksheets; the game works either way.
3. Assign the event the teams are to work on.
4. Give one **Worksheet** copy to each team member.
5. While they are playing, if it seems appropriate, give the teams brief breaks in the questioning process to confer among themselves.

Directions to Students

You have a **Counter Questions Worksheet**. Based on the event explained at the top of the sheet, you must do the following:

1. Work with your teammates. Using the framework provided by the worksheet, determine the characters and circumstances of the event. *Note:* When determining the characters and circumstances of an event, you must know enough about them to be able to answer any reasonable questions. For example, if the event requires the name of a country, your team should not choose a country if you don't know where it is or what language its citizens speak. Likewise, the characters you choose should be people known to other members of the class, such as other students, teachers, or famous world figures.
2. So that every player gets a turn to ask questions, set up an order of rotation listing who will ask questions in what order.
3. Toss a coin to determine which team begins the questioning.
4. The teacher may allow your team to pause and stop the questioning for a short time in order to consult and discuss your questions and answers.

Rules

1. Only yes/no questions may be asked. Questions should be answered with complete sentences, as you would give to a lawyer or to the police: "Yes, I saw a man in a red hat." Do not ask questions to confirm your guess: "Is this person Juan?"
2. When a player receives a yes answer, the next questioner in the order of rotation from that same team asks their questions. When a player receives a no answer, the opposing team begins its questioning round.
3. To win, your team must discover all the information about the other team's event. Don't announce your discoveries until you believe your team has all the information.

THE CRIME

Someone has committed a crime. Your task is to uncover the crime, the criminal, the victim, the motive, the weapon, and the scene of the crime.

CRIME:

CRIMINAL:

VICTIM:

MOTIVE:

WEAPON:

SCENE:

THE TUTOR

Someone is tutoring someone else in a particular subject. Your task is to discover the tutor, the person being tutored, the subject, the place and the time of the tutoring session.

TUTOR:

TUTOR'S PUPIL:

SUBJECT MATTER:

PLACE:

TIME:

THE SPORTS INJURY

Two athletes are competing against each other in a sport. One of them is injured. Your task is to discover the sport, the two athletes (two players or team captains), the winner, the injured athlete (one of the two named athletes), and the type of injury.

ATHLETE #1:

ATHLETE #2:

SPORT:

WINNER:

INJURED ATHLETE:

INJURY:

Section: Yes/No Questions

THE GIFT

A person bought someone a gift for a special occasion. Your task is to discover the gift-giver, the recipient, the gift, the color and the price of the gift, and the occasion or the reason for the gift.

GIFT-GIVER:

RECIPIENT:

GIFT:

COLOR:

PRICE:

OCCASION:

THE ACCIDENT

Two people were involved in an accident. Your task is to discover the kind of accident, the location where it occurred, the two people involved, the injured person, the part of the body that was injured, and the person who was at fault.

KIND OF ACCIDENT:

LOCATION:

PERSON #1:

PERSON #2:

INJURED PERSON:

INJURY:

PERSON AT FAULT:

         Section: Yes/No Questions

Roommate Search

Language Focus

Yes/no questions, vocabulary.

Summary of Game

Students establish their own criteria for a compatible roommate, then question their classmates to find the best candidate.

Number of Players

Any number.

Preparation by Teacher

Before Class
Make a copy of the **Roommate Search** survey for each student.

Directions to Students

1. Your goal is to find someone to share an apartment with. You want to find a compatible person.
2. First, think about the kind of roommate you want. Complete the left side of the **Roommate Search** survey form: "My ideal roommate should ..." Consider each pair of statements (for instance, "like pets/have no pets"), and put a check-mark after the phrase that better expresses your view.
3. Use the first two statements in the section marked "A" to form questions that you can ask of *everyone* in the class. This will help you eliminate the students who are not compatible in those two areas.
4. Then interview the students you didn't eliminate on the remaining points in the section marked "B." Put their names in the boxes at the top of the chart on the right. Then, as you interview, put check-marks in the boxes below the names of the people who agree with your views.
5. When you have finished your survey, add up the check-marks to see which classmate would be the best roommate for you.

ROOMMATE SEARCH SURVEY FORM

My ideal roommate should...		PROSPECTIVE CANDIDATES' NAMES							
A be a non-smoker ___	tolerate smoking ___								
want a male roommate ___	want a female roommate ___								
B be a morning person ___	be a night person ___								
be wild and fun-loving ___	be quiet and reserved ___								
be very neat ___	not be fussy about neatness ___								
be willing to share things ___	not use my things ___								
like pets ___	have no pets ___								
not put a lot of emphasis on clothes ___	be well-groomed and stylish ___								
be willing to share problems and listen to my problems ___	respect my privacy ___								
socialize with my friends and me ___	be independent and enjoy being alone ___								
want to do chores together ___	want to do chores independently ___								
be willing to share food ___	not eat any of my food ___								

Section: Yes/No Questions

Kitchen Clutter

Language Focus

Yes/no questions, kitchen vocabulary. As a variation, tag questions.

Summary of Game

By asking one another yes/no questions, students find out what **Kitchen Object** they represent.

Number of Players

4–27. (There are 27 kitchen objects described.)

Preparation by Teacher

Before Class
1. Make a copy of **Kitchen Object Tags.**
2. Cut out the tags so that you have one for each player.

In Class
Tape a **Kitchen Object Tag** to each player's back without letting the player see what is printed on the tag.

Directions to Students

1. On your backs are tags with the names of some of the many objects that can be found cluttering up a typical American kitchen.
2. Circulate among your classmates. Let them read your **Kitchen Object Tag**.
3. Ask yes/no questions to discover the name of your object. You may not ask direct questions such as "Is this a can-opener?" Instead, ask questions like these: "Is this made of metal?" "Is this usually kept in a drawer?" "Do I usually hold this in my hand when I'm eating?"
4. Ask and answer only one question of each classmate and then move on to another player.
5. After 10 minutes, try to guess what your object is.

Variation

Use yes/no tag questions and short answers. Practice both negative and positive tags and answers:

> **"My object is made of metal, isn't it?"**
> *or*
> **"My object isn't made of metal, is it?"**
>
> **"No, it isn't.**
> *or*
> **"Yes, it is."**

REFRIGERATOR	COOKBOOK	TRASH CAN
FOOD PROCESSOR	TOASTER	DISHWASHING LIQUID
SAUCER	MICROWAVE OVEN	ALUMINUM FOIL
OVEN	SUGAR	SINK
COFFEE MAKER	ROLLING PIN	SPATULA
MIXER	POT	BLENDER
COOKIE JAR	SALT SHAKER	ELECTRIC CAN OPENER
PAPER TOWELS	ORANGE JUICE	TABLESPOON
FRYING PAN	STOVE	TEASPOON

Section: Yes/No Questions

Zoo Are You?

Language Focus

Yes/no questions, animal vocabulary. As a variation, tag questions.

Summary of Game

By asking one another yes/no questions, students find out what animal they represent.

Number of Players

4–29. (There are 29 animals described.)

Preparation by Teacher

Before Class
1. Make a copy of **Animal Tags**.
2. Cut out the tags so that you have one for each player.

In Class
Tape an **Animal Tag** to each player's back without letting the player see what is printed on the tag.

Directions to Students

1. You're all animals in this activity. Your "animal identity" is printed on the card taped to your back.
2. Circulate among your classmates. Let them read your **Animal Tag**.
3. Ask yes/no questions to find out what animal you represent. You may not ask direct questions like "Am I a giraffe?" Instead, ask such questions as, "Am I a domestic animal? "Am I a four-legged animal?" "Am I a good swimmer?" "Am I found in cold climates?" Vary your answers. Sometimes respond fully: "No, I'm not a good swimmer," and sometimes more briefly: "No, I'm not."
4. Ask and answer only one question of each classmate before moving on to another student.
5. After 10 minutes, try to guess which animal you are.

Variation

Use yes/no tag questions and short answers. Practice both negative and positive tags and long and short answers:

> **"I'm a good swimmer, am I not?"**
> *or*
> **"I'm not a good swimmer, am I?"**

> **"No, you're not a good swimmer."**
> *or*
> **"Yes, you are."**

ELEPHANT	DEER	BEAR
SQUIRREL	PIG	SHARK
OSTRICH	COW	CAMEL
LIZARD	KANGAROO	DONKEY
WHALE	PANDA	MOUSE
RABBIT	TIGER	RACCOON
ZEBRA	CHIMPANZEE	POSSUM
SNAKE	PANTHER	GORILLA
BAT	PORPOISE	FOX

101   *Section: Yes/No Questions*

Relatively Speaking

Language Focus

Yes/no questions, vocabulary of the family. As a variation, tag questions.

Summary of Game

By asking one another yes/no questions, students find out how they're related to an imaginary person.

Number of Players

4–18. (There are 18 relationships described. For classes larger than 18, two groups may be formed.)

Preparation by Teacher

Before Class
1. Make one copy or more of **Relationship Tags**. Cut them out so that you have a tag for each player.
2. Make a copy of the **Family Tree** for each group.

In Class
Tape a **Relationship Tag** to each player's back without letting the player see what is printed on the tag.

Directions to Students

1. You're all related to a fictional character, Ms. Smith, but you don't know your relationship. It's printed on the tag taped on your back.
2. Circulate among your classmates. Let them read your **Relationship Tag**.
3. Ask yes/no questions to discover your relationship. You may not ask direct questions such as "Am I Ms. Smith's grandmother?" Instead, ask questions like these: "Am I a man?" "Am I of the same generation as Ms. Smith?" "Am I married to her uncle?" "Am I a blood relative?" "Am I related by marriage?" Answer questions fully: "No, you are not married to her uncle."
4. Ask each classmate player one question and answer only one. Then move on to another player.
5. At the end of the activity, go to the front of the class and fill in your name on the **Family Tree.** As the tree fills up with names, you will see if you have guessed your relationship correctly. When the tree is full, check to be sure you are right by looking at the tag on your back.

Variation

Use yes/no tag questions and full answers:

> **"I am Ms. Smith's grandmother, am I not?"**

> **"No, you're not. You're not her grandmother."**
> *or*
> **"Yes, you are. You are her grandmother."**

Relatively Speaking Relationship Tags

MS. SMITH'S UNCLE (HER FATHER'S BROTHER)	MS. SMITH'S MOTHER
MS. SMITH'S FATHER	MS. SMITH'S GRANDFATHER
MS. SMITH'S SISTER-IN-LAW (HER BROTHER'S WIFE)	MS. SMITH'S NIECE (HER BROTHER'S DAUGHTER)
MS. SMITH'S COUSIN (HER AUNT'S DAUGHTER)	MS. SMITH'S SISTER-IN-LAW (HER HUSBAND'S SISTER)
MS. SMITH'S SON-IN-LAW (HER DAUGHTER'S HUSBAND)	MS. SMITH'S NEPHEW (HER BROTHER'S SON)
MS. SMITH'S AUNT (HER FATHER'S SISTER)	MS. SMITH'S UNCLE (HER MOTHER'S BROTHER)
MS. SMITH'S GREAT-AUNT (HER GRANDMOTHER'S SISTER)	MS. SMITH'S BROTHER
MS. SMITH'S HUSBAND	MS. SMITH'S SISTER
MS. SMITH'S BROTHER-IN-LAW (HER SISTER'S HUSBAND)	MS. SMITH'S GREAT-UNCLE (HER GRANDMOTHER'S BROTHER)

The Smith Family Tree

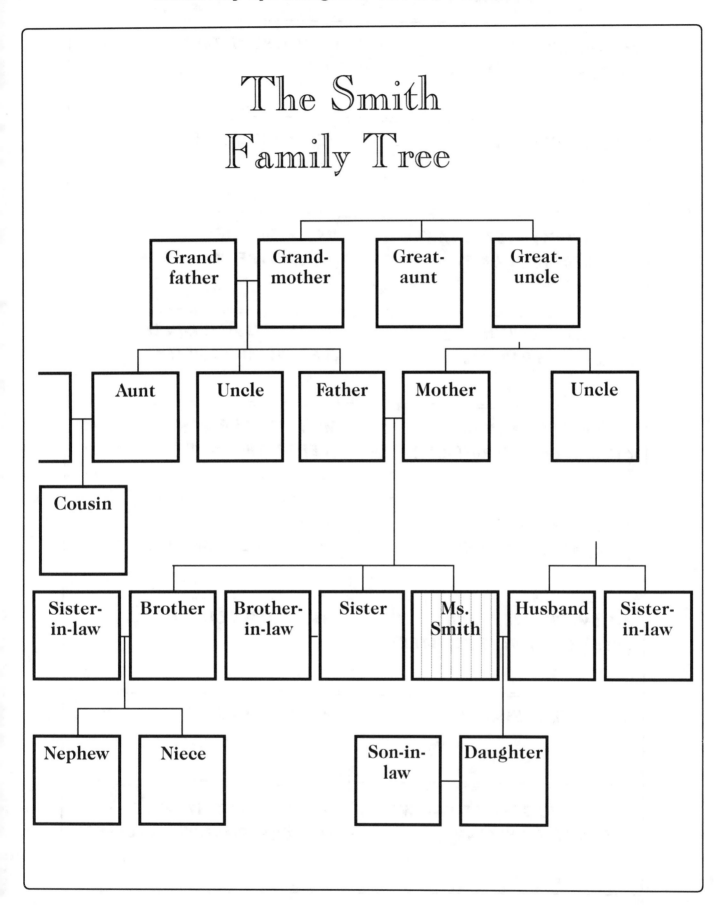

Such a Good Time!

Language Focus

Such ... that and *so ... that.*

Summary of Game

Students put together sentence fragments to form complete sentences with **such ... that** or **so ... that.**

Individual Format

Number of Players

Minimum of 12.

Preparation by Teacher

Before Class
1. Duplicate the **Sentence Fragments** sheet. Cut it up so that you have 24 slips.
2. Put enough slips in a box so that there will be one fragment for each player. There are 3 fragments for each of 8 sentences. Since the game depends on each player having a fragment and the fragments adding up to complete sentences, if your class is not divisible by 3, you will need to write and add one or two sentence fragments so that each player has one. You will then have one or two four-part sentences—for example, "I had such/a great time dancing/[until the prom ended at midnight]/ that my feet have blisters!" You would have written and added the [*until ...*] fragment.

In Class
1. When three players have found one another and formed a correct sentence, ask them to write it on the board and discard their fragments.
2. Have the other players put their slips of paper in the box again and scramble them. Add the fragments for an additional sentence so that the winners of the first round can keep playing.
3. Have all the players draw again.

Directions to Students

Each of you has a slip of paper containing part of a sentence. Find two (or three) classmates whose fragments, when added to yours, make a complete, logical sentence. When you have found them, bring your sentence to the blackboard. If it is correct, you will write it there

Group Format

Number of Players

Minimum of 4.

Preparation by Teacher

Before Class
1. Determine how many teams you're going to have.
2. Duplicate one set of **Sentence Fragments** sheet for each team.
3. Cut the sheets up into 24 slips, keeping the slips from each sheet separate as a set. To avoid confusion, you might want to use a different color of paper for each team.

In Class
Divide the class into teams and give one set of **Sentence Fragments** to each team.

Directions to Students

Each team has a set of **Sentence Fragments**. Your task is to arrange your fragments into complete and logical sentences. The first team to use up all of its fragments making sentences wins. *Note:* To make the "group format" a little easier, tell the players that each sentence is broken into three fragments.

Ken has so
many problems in math class
that he needs to see the teacher for help
Lassie is such
a good dog
that she never growls
Tammy is so
tall
that she can reach the ceiling without jumping
Carlos and Toshi are such
good friends
that they never argue
Samuel made so
much money at his job
that he bought a new convertible
Our state had so
little rain last year
that a lot of crops were ruined
The movie was so
sad
that a lot of people in the audience cried
This restaurant serves such
delicious food
that it's always crowded

 Section: So/Such ... That

Too Old to Be So Poor

Language Focus

Too and *enough.*

Summary of Game

On the basis of clues (all of which include *too* or *enough*) learned from classmates, students try to figure out two facts about a fictional character named Ron: how old he is and how much money he has in his pocket.

Number of Players

6–21.

Preparation by Teacher

Before Class
1. Duplicate the list of 21 **Clues**.
2. Cut it up into slips

In Class
Distribute the **Clues** as evenly as possible among the players. Depending on the class size, each player will have from 1 to 3 **Clues**. Ask them to memorize their **Clue(s)** and then put them away.

Directions to Students

1. You have **Clues** concerning Ron's age and the amount of money he has in his pocket.
2. Circulate among your classmates and, by listening to their **Clues**, try to decide how old Ron is and how much money he has. (**Hint:** Ron is in the United States and has only dollar bills in his pocket.)
3. The student wins who comes closest to guessing Ron's age and the amount of money in his pocket.

Solution

Ron is 20 years old and has $5 in his pocket.

| Ron is old enough to drive. |
| Ron is old enough to vote. |
| Ron is too young to retire. |
| Ron is too young to be the president of the United States. |
| Ron isn't old enough to drink liquor legally in all states. |
| Ron is old enough to work full-time. |
| Ron is old enough to join the armed services. |
| Ron is old enough to see an R-rated movie. |
| Ron is too young to teach someone to drive. |
| Ron is too young to be a grandparent. |
| Ron is too old to pay the children's ticket price at the zoo. |
| Ron doesn't have enough money to go to a first-run evening movie. |
| Ron doesn't have enough money to buy a CD. |
| Ron has enough money to buy a hamburger and a small cola at a fast-food restaurant. |
| Ron doesn't have enough money to buy a pair of dress shoes. |
| Ron has enough money to buy a copy of *Newsweek*. |
| Ron has enough money to go to a bargain movie matinee. |
| Ron has too little money to buy a tire for his mom's car. |
| Ron has enough money to buy a bag of potato chips. |
| Ron doesn't have enough money to buy a pair of jeans. |
| Ron doesn't have enough money to buy a book of 20 postage stamps. |

Three-Legged Race

Language Focus

Transitions (*but, therefore, on the other hand,* etc.).

Summary of Game

Students arrange sentence fragments into complete sentences, each with a transitional word or phrase.

Individual Format (appropriate for smaller classes)

Number of Players

3–21, preferably a number divisible by 3.

Preparation by Teacher

Before Class
1. Make a copy of the **Sentence Fragments** sheet (page 112). Cut out the fragments, putting aside the slips of paper at the bottom of the page that contain only punctuation marks; they will not be used in this format. Note that without punctuation, each of the 7 correct sentences will have 3 parts, making 21 slips.
2. Choose appropriate **Sentence Fragments**, so that each student in the class will receive one slip, and only correct sentences will be formed, each with 3 parts. Put the slips in a box.

In Class
Have each player draw one slip without looking.

Directions to Students

1. This is a race. Each of you has one-third of a sentence. The object is to find the other two students with the rest of your sentence.
2. When you have found them, the three of you should inform the teacher and write your sentence on the board *with the correct punctuation*. If the sentence is correct, you win the race.

Note to Teacher

If you didn't use all the fragments in the game (i.e., if your class is smaller than 21 students), you can repeat the activity after the first 3 students have won the race by removing the 3 winning fragments, adding 3 new ones, and having the other students put their fragments back in the box. Have the students draw again.

Group Format (appropriate for a class of any size)

Number of Players

Any number.

Preparation by Teacher

Before Class
1. Determine how many teams you're going to have. Teams should be of equal size.
2. Make a copy of the **Sentence Fragments** sheet for each team.
3. Cut out the fragments. For each team, you'll now have a set of fragments (3 per complete sentence) and a set of punctuation marks. Shuffle each set, keeping the two sets separate.
4. Arrange seats so that each team is in a circle.

In Class
Place a shuffled set of fragments and a shuffled set of punctuation marks in the center of each circle.

Directions to Students

In the center of your circle there are 7 sentences, each divided into 3 fragments. Each sentence requires punctuation. Your task is to work together to assemble the sentences, including punctuation, as quickly as possible. The first team to assemble all the sentences correctly wins.

Three-Legged Race Sentence Fragments

because	she had a map	she didn't get lost
in spite of	getting good directions	she got lost
she hadn't gotten directions	but	she was still able to find the concert hall
Susi didn't study for the test	therefore	she failed it
Susi isn't a bad student	on the contrary	she usually gets A's
Betty failed the test	despite	studying for five hours
Susi usually gets A's on her tests	on the other hand	Betty usually gets C's

,	,	;	.	,	.	,
.	.	,	;	.	;	.

Red Rover 1: What Am I Doing?

Language Focus

Present continuous tense.

Summary of Game

In order to join a team, students have to guess what someone is doing by that person's oral clues and name the action using the present continuous tense. Each team tries to get more people than the other.

Number of Players

Any number. There are 27 activities.

Preparation by Teacher

Before Class
Make 2 copies of **Red Rover Activities**.

In Class
1. Choose, or have the class choose, two team leaders to start the action. (They should be two of the more verbal students.)
2. Give each leader a copy of **Red Rover Activities**.
3. Have the leaders stand at opposite sides of the room, with the rest of the class in the middle.

Directions to Students

1. The two team leaders have a list of **Red Rover Activities**. We will toss a coin to determine who begins the game.
2. The winner of the coin toss:
    a. chooses an activity from the list. (All verbs are in the simple continuous (sometimes called progressive) tense—for example, *drying the dishes.*)
    b. thinks of three separate actions that would be part of that general activity (*pick up a wet plate, rub it with a cloth, put it in a rack*).
    c. calls on a classmate (not the other captain).
    d. gives clues to the activity by describing the three separate actions. The descriptions can't contain any of the words already used in the chosen phrase. For *drying the dishes*, for example, the captain can't use the words *drying* or *dishes.*
3. If the chosen player guesses the activity and uses the present continuous tense to make a correct sentence ("Maria is drying the dishes."), that player comes over to the side of the leader who gave the clues and becomes the new leader, giving the next clues. The new leader and all the old leaders on that team can consult on how to describe the activities.
4. The second captain repeats the process.
5. The teams take turns until there are no more players left in the middle of the room or there are no more phrases on the list.
6. The larger team at the end of the game wins.

Note: The game is easier if gestures are allowed, more difficult if only words are permitted.

Example of a Typical Exchange

The leader chooses "changing the oil in a car."
The leader calls on Saed and says:

"I'm opening a plug under the vehicle.
I'm letting the black liquid drain out.
I'm putting new black liquid under the hood of the vehicle.
Saed, what am I doing?"

If Saed responds correctly with, "You're changing the oil in a car," he joins the leader's team.

baking a cake	changing a tire	fishing
making an appointment	writing a letter	washing a car
taking a shower	playing a video game	playing baseball
riding a bike	painting a picture	flying a kite
getting a driver's license	watching a parade	cooking a hamburger
reading a newspaper	listening to the radio	packing a suitcase
cleaning house	taking a test	eating pizza
washing dishes	washing hair	reading a letter
going camping	getting dressed	cashing a check

Red Rover 2: What Did You Do?

Language Focus

Simple past tense.

Summary of Game

Students join a team by answering a question correctly using verbs in the simple past tense. Each team tries to get more people that the other.

Number of Players

Any number.

Preparation by Teacher

Before Class
Make two copies of **Simple Past Verbs**.

In Class
1. Choose, or have the class choose, two team leaders to start the action. (They should be two of the more verbal students.)
2. Give each leader a copy of **Simple Past Verbs**.
3. Have the leaders stand at opposite sides of the room, with the rest of the class in the middle.

Directions to Students

1. The two team leaders have a list of **Simple Past Verbs**. We will toss a coin to determine who begins the game.
2. The winner of the coin toss:
    a. chooses a verb from the list.
    b. thinks of a question that will get an answer using the chosen simple past verb (the question can't contain any form of that verb).
    c. calls on a classmate—not the other team captain.
    d. asks the question.
3. If the chosen player answers correctly, using the simple past tense, that player comes over to the side of the leader who asked the question and becomes the new leader asking the next. The new leader and all the old leaders on that team can work together to think of the next question.
4. The second leader repeats the process.
5. The teams take turns until there are no more players left in the middle of the room or there are no more verbs on the list.
6. The larger team at the end of the game wins.

Example of a Typical Exchange

The leader chooses the verb *drove*.
The leader calls on Saed and asks, "Saed, how did you get here today?"
If Saed replies with a sentence containing *drove*, such as "I *drove*," or "My friend *drove* me," he joins that leader's team.
If he replies with a different verb—for example, "I *came* by car," or "I *walked*," or if he uses any other tense, such as "I *was driving* to school today," he has to stay in the middle of the room.

     116

Red Rover 2
Simple Past Verbs

ate	washed	watched
called	brushed	drank
went	read	lent
wrote	forgot	rode
took	sent	gave
made	rang	broke
opened	closed	stopped
flew	sang	bought
saw	won	lost
told	lied	ran
left	came	finished
found	asked	sat
slept	waited	fell
laughed	borrowed	followed
slipped	chased	licked

What Do We Have in Common?

Language Focus

Questions and statements in simple present tense; *both* and *neither ... nor.*

Summary of Game

Students try to find classmates with whom they have things in common, both positive and negative.

Number of Players

Any number.

Preparation by Teacher

Before Class
Make one copy of the two pages of the **Report Sheet** for each student.

In Class
Distribute copies of the **Report Sheet**.

Directions to Students

1. You're going to find out what you and your classmates have in common. Look at your **Report Sheets**. Notice that you can state what you have in common with affirmative sentences using *both* or with negative sentences using *neither ... nor*.
2. Think of some facts about yourself, such as things you like and don't like, things you can and can't do.
3. Using those facts, circulate among your classmates and ask them questions until you discover something that you have in common. Use the present tense.
4. Write what you have in common on your **Report Sheet**.
5. Question as many of your classmates as you can in 20 minutes. Then you'll tell us about your discoveries.

What Do We Have in Common?
REPORT SHEET

Classmate		Thing in common
Example: **Budi**	and I both	*know how to swim.*
_____	and I both	_____
_____	and I both	_____
_____	and I both	_____
_____	and I both	_____
_____	and I both	_____
_____	and I both	_____
_____	and I both	_____
_____	and I both	_____
_____	and I both	_____
_____	and I both	_____
_____	and I both	_____
_____	and I both	_____
_____	and I both	_____
_____	and I both	_____
_____	and I both	_____
_____	and I both	_____
_____	and I both	_____
_____	and I both	_____
_____	and I both	_____
_____	and I both	_____

What Do We Have in Common?
REPORT SHEET

Classmate		Thing in common

Example:

Neither _____Yolanda_____ nor I _like cafeteria food._

Neither _____ nor I _____

Neither _____ nor I _____

Neither _____ nor I _____

Neither _____ nor I _____

Neither _____ nor I _____

Neither _____ nor I _____

Neither _____ nor I _____

Neither _____ nor I _____

Neither _____ nor I _____

Neither _____ nor I _____

Neither _____ nor I _____

Neither _____ nor I _____

Neither _____ nor I _____

Neither _____ nor I _____

Neither _____ nor I _____

Neither _____ nor I _____

Neither _____ nor I _____

Neither _____ nor I _____

Neither _____ nor I _____

Neither _____ nor I _____

Crystal Ball

Language Focus

Simple future with *will*.

Summary of Game

Students make predictions about their classmates' future, based on present observations.

Number of Players

Any number.

Preparation by Teacher

Before Class
1. Make a copy of the **Predictions Report Form** (page 122) for each player.
2. Write the name of each player on a slip of paper and place the slips in a box.

In Class
Distribute copies of the **Predictions Report Form**.

Directions to Students

1. Each of you will draw the name of a class member from the box. This will be the *Subject* of your predictions; you will be called the *Predictor.* It's O.K. if you draw your own name.
2. Make a prediction about your *Subject,* the person whose name you drew, and give a reason for the prediction. Substitute the words *this person* for your *Subject*'s name and any personal pronoun— for example, "This person will own a candy store someday because this person eats more candy than anyone else I know," or "This person will be an accountant because this person is very, very neat."
3. Talk to one classmate at a time. Each person you talk to will listen to your prediction and tell you theirs—*be careful not to give away your Subject's name.*
4. When other students tell you their predictions, fill in their names under *Predictor* and their predictions under *Prediction* on the **Predictions Report Form**.
5. Under *Subject* put the name of the person you guess the *Predictor* is talking about.
6. When everyone has heard all the predictions, you will have the chance to see how many correct guesses you made.

Note: Depending on the size of your class, you may prefer to set a time limit rather than have the students gather the predictions of all the other players. Announce the time limit before the game begins.

The Crystal Ball

Predictions Report Form

Predictor	Subject	Prediction
_____says that	_____	_____
_____says that	_____	_____
_____says that	_____	_____
_____says that	_____	_____
_____says that	_____	_____
_____says that	_____	_____
_____says that	_____	_____
_____says that	_____	_____
_____says that	_____	_____
_____says that	_____	_____
_____says that	_____	_____
_____says that	_____	_____
_____says that	_____	_____
_____says that	_____	_____
_____says that	_____	_____
_____says that	_____	_____
_____says that	_____	_____
_____says that	_____	_____
_____says that	_____	_____
_____says that	_____	_____
_____says that	_____	_____
_____says that	_____	

Section: Verbs　　　　122

Time Line

Language Focus

Future perfect and future perfect continuous tenses.

Summary of Game

Using clues and a time line, students complete sentences (in future perfect tenses) about fictional "Johnny."

Number of Players

Any number, divided into groups of 10 (or smaller, with some students then being given more than one clue, so that all 10 clues are used).

Preparation by Teacher

Before Class
1. Make one copy each of the **Time Line** and the **Report Sheet** for each student.
2. Make a copy of **Clues** and cut them out.

In Class
Give each student a **Clue**, a copy of the **Time Line**, and a copy of the **Report Sheet**.

Directions to Students

1. Each of you has a sentence **Clue** about an event in Johnny's life. You also have a **Time Line** and a **Report Sheet**.
2. Circulate, telling each other your **Clues**. On your **Time Line**, fill in each clue you hear.
3. When you have collected all the clues and filled in your **Time Line**, complete your **Report Sheet**.
4. The first person to complete the **Report Sheet** correctly wins.

In 1995, Johnny started to learn English.

Johnny first played the guitar in 1990.

In 2000, Johnny moved to Columbus, Ohio.

Johnny will become a doctor in 2010.

In 2015, Johnny will move to Florida.

In 2002, Johnny began medical school.

Johnny joined a yacht club in 1997, and he remained a member the rest of his life.

In 2012, Johnny will get married.

Johnny first sang in the choir in 1998.

Johnny has been supporting his mother since 2001.

TIME LINE

'90   '95   '97   '98   '2000   '03   '05   '10   '12   '15   '20   '30

Section: Verbs

TIME LINE
REPORT SHEET

1. By 2010, Johnny _____ for 15 years.

2. By 2010, Johnny _____ for 20 years.

3. By 2014, Johnny _____ for 14 years.

4. By 2020, Johnny _____ for 10 years.

5. By 2020, Johnny _____ for 5 years.

6. By 2007, Johnny _____ for 5 years.

7. By 2017, Johnny _____ for 20 years.

8. By 2030, Johnny _____ for 18 years.

9. By 2013, Johnny _____ for 15 years.

10. By 2021, Johnny _____ for 20 years.

Passive Developments

Language Focus

Future passive.

Summary of Game

Students share verbal clues (rumors) to draw a picture of landscape changes that will be brought about by a suburban development project.

Number of Players

5–15 (there are 15 clues).

Preparation by Teacher

Before Class
1. Make a copy of the **Before** picture for each student.
2. Make a single copy of **Rumors** and cut them out.
3. Each student will need a blank piece of 8 1/2" x 11" paper, a pencil, and an eraser.

In Class
1. Give each student a **Rumor** and a **Before** picture.
2. Be sure everyone has the other necessary supplies.

Directions to Students

1. You have a **Before** picture of a 200-acre tract of land outside Grammarville, U.S.A. A construction company plans to develop it, and you and your classmates have heard various **Rumors** about the changes that will be made.
2. Circulate, telling each other the **Rumors** you've heard. Your conversation may sound like this:

   A. I've heard a rumor that an addition will be built onto the east end of the old farm-house.
   B. Really? They say that the foot bridge will be removed, too.

3. On the basis of all the **Rumors** you gather, draw a sketch of what the completed project will look like.
4. When you're finished, compare your sketch with the official plans of the chief engineer, your teacher.

127

The barn will be torn down.

The tree beside the stream will be cut down.

The stone wall will be removed.

The trees to the west will be cut down.

The hill to the west of the barn will be leveled.

A high-rise apartment building will be built in the northeast corner.

The water tower to the northwest will be replaced by a school.

The foot bridge will be removed.

A road bisecting the community from the southwest to the northeast will be constructed.

The pine forest in the north will be replaced by a development of four houses.

A picnic table will be placed on the north bank of the stream.

Flowers will be planted along the south bank of the brook.

A flagpole will be erected in front of the school.

An addition will be built onto the east end of the old farmhouse.

The front and side porches will be taken off the house.

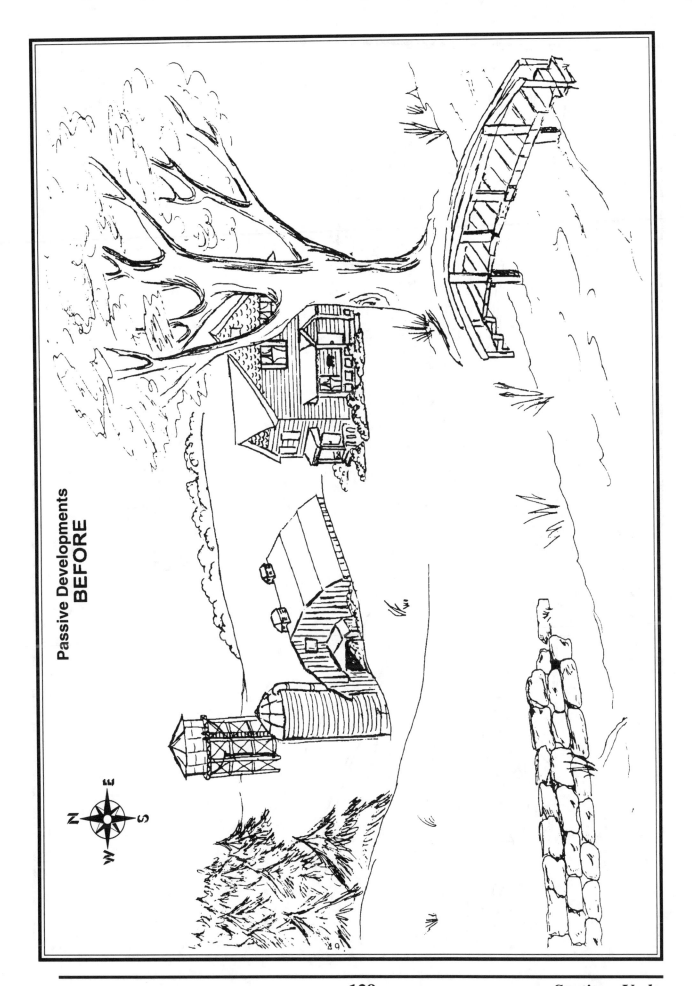

Passive Developments
BEFORE

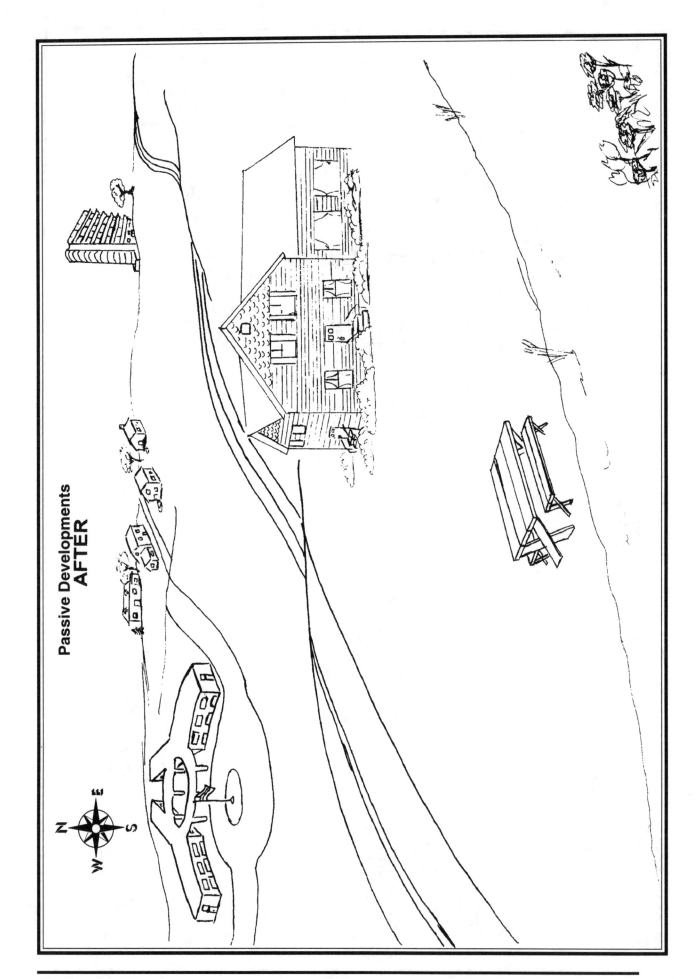

Passive Developments
AFTER

Survey of Experience

Language Focus

Present perfect tense.

Summary of Game

Students circulate and find out whether their classmates have had the listed experiences.

Number of Players

Any number.

Preparation by Teacher

Before Class
Make a copy of either the **Activity List 1** or **2** for each student. Make an equal number of each list.

In Class
Distribute the copies to your students.

Directions to Students

1. You'll have 10 minutes to get as many signatures on your **Activity List** as you can.
2. Circulate, asking your classmates questions based on items in the list, such as "Have you ever bought an airplane?"
3. Your classmate answers truthfully, "Yes, I have," or "No, I haven't." If their answer shows that they are the person the **Activity List** tells you to find, have them sign next to the appropriate item.
4. The player with the most signatures after 10 minutes wins.

Example of a Typical Exchange

Start with an activity from the **Activity List** (This example isn't from the list.):

hasn't taken a subway in the last year.

Your question: **Have you taken a subway in the last year?**
Classmate 1: **Yes, I have.**
You: **Thank you, but that isn't the answer I am looking for.**

You ask another classmate: **Have you taken a subway in the last year?**
Classmate 2: **No, I haven't.**
You: **Great. Please sign my list here.**

Survey of Experience
Activity List

Find someone who...	Name
1. has changed a diaper	_____
2. has changed the oil in a car.	_____
3. has never eaten with chopsticks.	_____
4. has been to Disney World.	_____
5. has broken an arm or a leg.	_____
6. has been on TV.	_____
7. has written a letter within the last two weeks.	_____
8. has gotten an American driver's license.	_____
9. has ridden in a taxi.	_____
10. has been to an American zoo.	_____
11. has eaten corn on the cob.	_____
12. has never ridden on a Ferris wheel.	_____
13. has ice-skated.	_____
14. has already used a dictionary today.	_____
15. has seen a movie in the past week.	_____
16. hasn't chewed bubble gum in the last two years.	_____
17. has climbed a tree.	_____

Survey of Experience
Activity List

Find someone who...   **Name**

1. has read a novel in the last month.   _____

2. has gone to an opera.   _____

3. has never eaten clams.   _____

4. has been robbed.   _____

5. hasn't seen a Star Wars movie.   _____

6. has ridden a camel or a donkey.   _____

7. hasn't eaten at a McDonald's in the last year.   _____

8. has never owned a pet.   _____

9. has walked five blocks today.   _____

10. has been to an American museum.   _____

11. has never swum in the ocean.   _____

12. has never been to a circus.   _____

13. has spoken to a parent this past week.   _____

14. has already had a glass of milk today.   _____

15. has slept out doors at least once.   _____

16. hasn't watched TV in the last two days.   _____

17. has never wanted to play a musical instrument. _____

Carol's Day

Language Focus

Past perfect tense.

Summary of Game

Students number a series of pictures in the correct sequence, according to statements given by other students.

Number of Players

Version A: 6–9. Version B: 10–16.

Preparation by Teacher

There are two versions of this game. **Version A** includes 6 **Pictures** of Carol's activities and 9 **Statements** about those activities. The first 6 **Statements** are sufficient to complete the sequencing of the activities. **Version B** includes the same 6 activities plus an additional 3 activities, for a total of 9 **Pictures** and 16 **Statements** about those activities. The first 10 **Statements** are sufficient to complete the sequencing. For larger classes, divide the class into groups of 6–9 students for **Version A**, or 10–16 students for **Version B.**

Before Class
1. Determine whether you're going to use **Version A** or **Version B**.
2. Make one copy of the appropriate **Pictures** (**A** or **B**) for each player.
3. Make one copy of the appropriate set of **Statements** and cut them out. You need one **Statement** for each player. Be sure to use at least the first 6 of **A** or 10 of **B**.

In Class
Give each student a page of **Pictures** and a **Statement**.

Directions to Students

1. Each of you has a **Statement** about Carol's day and a series of pictures that illustrate her day's activities.
2. Memorize your **Statement**. Circulate, exchanging statements with your classmates.
3. From the information you gather, number the pictures in the correct time sequence.
4. The first student to sequence the pictures correctly wins.

Solution (in Chronological order)

1. Carol wrote checks to pay bills.
2. Carol watched television.
3. Carol played golf.
4. Carol had her hair cut.
5. Carol took a shower.
6. Carol spoke to her friend on the phone.
*7. Carol went to the library.
*8. Carol ate lunch.
*9. Carol washed her car.

*These three activities are in **Version B** only.

━━━━━━━━━━

By the time she played golf, Carol had already written checks to pay her bills.

By the time Carol spoke to her friend on the phone, she had already had her hair cut and taken a shower.

Carol had already had her hair cut and played golf by the time she took a shower.

Carol had already played golf by the time she had her hair cut.

By the time Carol watched TV, she had already written checks to pay her bills.

By the time Carol played golf, she had already watched TV.

Carol had already paid her bills by the time she took a shower.

By the time she talked to her friend on the phone, Carol had already played golf.

Carol had already watched TV by the time she took a shower.

By the time she played golf, Carol had already written checks to pay her bills.

By the time Carol spoke to her friend on the phone, she had already had her hair cut and taken a shower.

Carol had already eaten lunch by the time she washed her car.

Carol had already played golf by the time she ate lunch.

By the time Carol took a shower, she had already had her hair cut and played golf.

By the time Carol went to the library, she had already spoken to her friend on the phone.

By the time Carol ate lunch, she had already gone to the library.

Carol had already played golf by the time she had her hair cut.

By the time Carol watched TV, she had already written checks to pay her bills.

Carol had already watched TV by the time she played golf.

By the time Carol went to the library, she had already watched TV.

By the time Carol took a shower, she had already paid her bills.

Carol had already played golf by the time she talked to her friend on the phone.

Carol had already written checks to pay her bills by the time she washed her car.

By the time she took a shower, Carol had already watched TV.

Carol had already visited the library by the time she washed her car.

Carol's Day
Version A

Section: Verbs

Carol's Day
Version B

Circle Chain

Language Focus

Past continuous.

Summary of Game

Students make statements about what they were doing at a certain time, repeating what everyone else in the chain has said before them, then adding their own statement.

Number of Players

Any number.

Preparation by Teacher

In Class
1. Have students sit in a circle.
2. Give students a minute to remember what they were doing yesterday evening at 8:00.
3. After giving instructions, appoint one student to begin.

Directions to Students

1. You'll have one minute to remember what you were doing yesterday evening at 8:00.
2. Then one player will be chosen to tell you what they were doing at that time.
3. The next player will repeat what the previous player was doing, using *while,* and add what he or she was doing.
4. Each player will repeat all of the previous player's activities and add their own.

Example of a Typical Pattern

Player A: I was watching television at 8:00 last night.
Player B: While (A's name) was watching television, I was reading the newspaper.
Player C: While (A's name) was watching TV and (B's name) was reading a newspaper, I was eating supper.

Ghost Story

Language Focus

Past continuous tense.

Summary of Game

Students find out what others were doing at a certain time, then complete a "ghost story" with those activities.

Number of Players

6 or more.

Preparation by Teacher

Before Class
Make a copy of the Report Form and the Ghost Story for each student.

Directions to Students

1. Think about what you were doing last night at 9:30.
2. Choose 6 classmates and ask them what they were doing last night at 9:30.
3. Complete your **Report Form** with their names and what they were doing. Remember to use the past continuous tense.
4. After you've filled out the **Report Form**, your teacher will give you a copy of the **Ghost Story**.
5. Write the names of the students you questioned, and their activities, in the appropriate blanks. For example, wherever it says *Student #1* and *Activity,* write the name of Student #1 and what they were doing, according to your **Report Form**.
6. You'll also have to circle *he* or *she* wherever the choice appears, so your story will read right.
7. Read the story. Your teacher may ask you to read it to the class.

GHOST STORY
REPORT FORM

"What were you doing last night at 9:30?"

Report the student's name and what the student was doing.

EXAMPLE: _Simi was writing a letter._

STUDENT #1: _____

STUDENT #2: _____

STUDENT #3: _____

STUDENT #4: _____

STUDENT #5: _____

STUDENT #6: _____

GHOST STORY

Last night as _____ _____, he/she suddenly saw a ghost outside
              student #1   activity

the window! Frightened, he/she called _____, who _____ at the
                                     student #2   activity

time. Being busy, he/she couldn't come over. In a panic, _____ ran over to
                                                 student #1

_____'s house shouting, "I've just seen a ghost!" _____, who
 student #3   student #3

_____, stopped what he/she was doing and tried to calm _____
   activity   student #1

down as he/she listened to _____'s story. "Let's investigate," suggested
                                 student #1

_____.
 student #3

        As they were walking briskly down the street, they passed by _____ as
                                                                   student #4

he/she _____. They laughed at him/her for wasting time that way. On
        activity

their way they stopped at _____'s house. They found _____ there too.
                    student #5   student #6

GHOST STORY, CONTINUED

_____ _____ while _____ _____. They
   student #5   activity   student #6   activity

stopped what they were doing and joined _____ and _____. Finally, all
                                             student #1   student #3

four of them arrived at _____'s house. They investigated the area outside the
                            student #1

window where _____ had seen the ghost. They discovered a sheet that had
                student #1

blown off the clothesline and become lodged in a bush outside the window. Because of

the wind, the sheet was moving, and it looked as though it was a ghost waving its

arms. Embarrassed, _____ joined the laughter of the others.
                student #1

Paul and Penny Played

Language Focus

Simple past, past perfect, and past continuous tenses.

Summary of Game

Using information gathered from classmates, students number pictures of Paul's and Penny's activities in correct chronological order.

Number of Players

7–16. (There are 16 **Statements**. For smaller groups, some players may be given two **Statements**.)

Preparation by Teacher

Before Class
1. Make a copy of the **Picture** of Paul's and Penny's activities for each player and one copy of the **Statements** sheet. (*Note:* The first 14 **Statements** are required for solving the puzzle. The last 2 are redundant and are included for larger classes.)
2. Cut up the sheet so that each player gets one or two **Statements.**

Directions to Students

1. You have 10 pictures showing activities in a day in the lives of Paul and Penny. While Paul was engaged in one activity, Penny was engaged in another.
2. You also have a **Statement** about their activities. Memorize your **Statement**.
3. Circulate among your classmates, telling one another your **Statements**.
4. Your goal is to number the activities of Paul from 1 to 5 and the *concurrent* activities of Penny from 1 to 5 according to the time order in which they happened.
5. The winner is the first student to number all 10 pictures in the correct chronological order.

Solution

1. Paul was painting a chair while Penny was playing soccer.
2. Paul shot pool with his friends while Penny went shopping with her friends.
3. Paul went bungee jumping while Penny was working in the garden.
4. Paul mailed a package while Penny was taking her *tae kwon do* lesson.
5. Paul was cooking dinner while Penny was reading the *Wall Street Journal.*

Penny wasn't playing soccer while Paul was shooting pool.

While Penny was reading the *Wall Street Journal*, Paul was cooking dinner.

Paul wasn't painting a chair while Penny was working in the garden.

While Paul was mailing a package, Penny was taking a *tae kwon do* lesson.

Penny wasn't shopping while Paul was bungee jumping.

When Paul went bungee jumping, Penny had already played soccer.

Paul had already shot pool with his friends when Penny took her *tae kwon do* lesson.

When Paul mailed a package, Penny had already played soccer.

Penny hadn't worked in the garden yet when Paul shot pool.

Penny had just finished her *tae kwon do* lesson before she read the *Wall Street Journal*.

When Paul shot pool, he had already painted the chair.

When Paul mailed the package, Penny had already worked in the garden.

Penny went shopping with friends immediately after she played soccer.

Paul had already gone bungee jumping when Penny took her *tae kwon do* lesson.

Penny had already stopped working in the garden by the time Paul was cooking dinner.

Paul had already painted the chair when Penny went shopping.

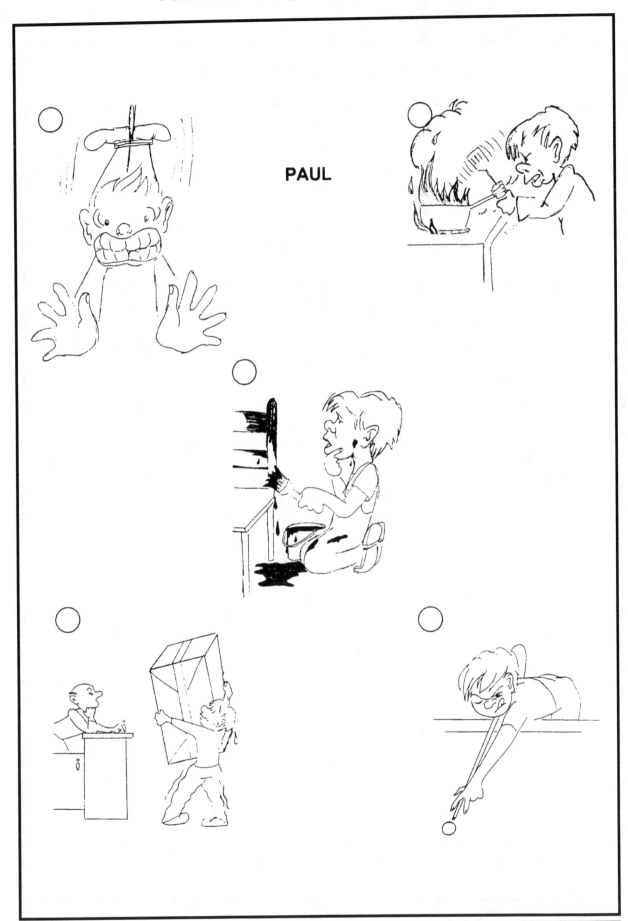

PAUL

PENNY

Search for Advice

Language Focus

Verbs and adjectives that are followed by the subjunctive.

Summary of Game

Each student finds the classmate who has the **Response** that matches his or her **Problem**.

Number of Players

6–14. There are 14 **Problems** and **Responses.**

Preparation by Teacher

Before Class
Duplicate the **Problems** and **Responses** and then cut them out.

In Class
Give a **Problem** and a non-matching **Response** to each player.

Directions to Students

1. Each of you has two slips of paper. One contains a **Problem** and the other contains a **Response** to a problem. The two don't match.
2. Your goal is to find the classmate whose **Response** does match your **Problem**.

Thanks for letting me use your lawnmower. Unfortunately, I broke it.

My brother just bought a new puppy. It keeps chewing on his shoes.

I have a terrible stomachache.

I've gained 10 pounds recently.

Now that Mrs. Smith's kids are grown, she wants to resume her career.

The baby just spilled grape juice on the carpet.

Bobby has a severe toothache.

Jill wants to go to college after high school.

Janet just had a fight with her boyfriend.

My neighbors play their stereo too loudly.

This town needs another library.

Mary's nephew is coming to visit her.

Tony makes attractive costume jewelry. He wants to sell it on the street.

My brand-new waterbed leaks.

I insist that you pay to have it fixed.

I suggest that he have it trained.

I recommend that you not eat raw onions anymore.

The coach insisted that you not be over 160 pounds to stay on the team.

I suggest that she see a career counselor.

It's essential that you clean it up before the stain sets.

It's essential that he see a dentist as soon as possible.

It's recommended that she take at least one science course.

I suggest they talk over their problems.

You should request that they turn it down.

The mayor has proposed that one be built on Main Street.

I suggest that she take him to the zoo.

The city requires that he have a vendor's license.

You should demand that the store replace it.

Index of Grammar and Vocabulary Topics

> **Grammar topics in Roman**
> *Vocabulary Topics in Italic*

151

Section: Verbs

Other materials from Pro Lingua:

Basic Series:

English Interplay *by Raymond C. Clark*

Games:

The Great Big BINGO Book *by Nina Ito and Anne Berry*

Pronunciation Card Games *by Linnea Henry*

Match It! *by Sharon Elwell and Raymond C. Clark*

The Interactive Tutorial, an Activity Parade *by Karen M. Sanders*

Play 'n Talk: Communicative Games for Elem./Middle School ESL *by Gordona Petricic*

Families: 10 Card Games *by Marjorie S. Fuchs, Jane Critchley, and Thomas Pyle.*

Index Card Games for ESL *edited by Raymond C. Clark*

More Index Card Games and Activities *by Raymond C. Clark*

Discovery Trail – an ESL/EFL board game or set of quiz cards *by Mark Feder*

Communicative Competence:

Do As I Say: 60 Operations in English *by Gayle Nelson, Thomas Winters, and R.C. Clark*

Conversation Strategies: Pair and Small Group Activities for Developing Communicative Competence *by David Kehe and Peggy Dustin Kehe.*

Discussion Strategies: Beyond Everyday Conversation *by David and Peggy Dustin Kehe.*

Conversation Inspirations: Over 2000 Conversation Topics *by Nancy Ellen Zelman*

Writing:

Writing Inspirations: A Fundex of Individualized Writing Activities *by Arlene Marcus*

Write for You: Creative Writing Activities *by Janet Morey and Gail Schafers*

Breaking the Writing Barrier: Activities for Adolescents *by Teryne Dorret*

Writing Strategies *by David Kehe and Peggy Dustin Kehe*

Others:

Lexicarry: Pictures for Learning Languages *by Patrick R. Moran*

Rhymes 'n Rhythms for the ESL Classroom *by Lisa Tenuta*

The Modal Book *by Joseph Krupp and Lisa Tenuta*

Conversation Surveys: Group Discussion and Journal Writing *by Deborah Hitsky*

Celebrating American Heroes: 13 Brief Plays on American History *by Anne Siebert*

Heroes from American History: An Intergrated Skills Reader *by A. Siebert and R.C. Clark*

Pearls of Wisdom: African and Caribbean Folktales *by Raouf Mama and Mary Romney*

For information about any of these materials or for a catalogue of all
the Pro Lingua publications, please visit our webstore at
www.ProLinguaAssociates.com, call 800 366 4775 or 802 257 7779,
fax 802 257 5117, email info@ProLinguaAssociates.com, or write to
Pro Lingua Associates, P.O. Box 1348, Brattleboro, Vermont 05302 U.S.A.